HEALTHIER CHOCOLATE TREATS

breakfasts, snacks & desserts
for every chocoholic

AMY ATHERTON

author of the blog *Amy's Healthy Baking*

Text and photographs Copyright © 2015 Amy Atherton. Design and Concept Copyright © 2015 Amy Atherton. All rights reserved. Any unauthorized duplication in whole or in part or dissemination of this edition by any means (including but not limited to photocopying, electronic devices, digital versions, and the Internet) will be prosecuted to the fullest extent of the law.

Published in the U.S. by
Ingram Content Group
1 Ingram Blvd
La Vergne, TN 37086
www.ingramspark.com

ISBN: 978-0-9895951-2-4

Printed in the United States by Ingram Content Group

10 9 8 7 6 5 4 3 2 1

Design and layout: Sarah Menanix
Photographs: © 2015 Amy Atherton

IMPORTANT NOTE TO READERS: This book is independently authored and published and no sponsorship or endorsement of this book by, and no affiliation with, any celebrities, trademarked brands or other products mentioned or pictured within is claimed or suggested. All trademarks that appear in directions, photographs, and elsewhere in this book belong to their respective owners and are used here for informational purposes only. The author encourages readers to patronize the quality brands and products mentioned and pictured in this book.

To my family and my guy, who always believed in me,
to my blog readers, whose support helped made this possible,
and to chocolate lovers everywhere.

TABLE OF CONTENTS

Introduction 7
Ingredients 9
Measurements 11
Equipment 12

BREAKFASTS 15
Strawberry Banana Chocolate Chip Muffins 16
Double Chocolate Zucchini Muffins . . . 18
Dark Chocolate Drizzled Blueberry Scones 20
Pumpkin Chocolate Chip Scones 23
Chocolate Chip Buttermilk Pancakes . . . 24
Banana French Toast with Chocolate Syrup 27
Strawberry & Dark Chocolate Sweet Rolls . 28
Chocolate Fudge Brownie Oatmeal 30
White Chocolate Berry Cheesecake
   Oatmeal 32
Dark Chocolate Cherry Granola 34
Dark Chocolate Cherry Yogurt Parfaits . . 37
White Chocolate Cinnamon Apple Coffee
   Cake 38
Chocolate Covered Strawberry Green
   Smoothie 40
Skinny Double Chocolate Frappuccino . . 42
Skinny Cookies 'n Cream Frappuccino . . 45

SNACKS 47
Chocolate Flax Crackers 48
Pumpkin Chocolate Chip Granola Bars . . 50
Dark Chocolate Blueberry Granola Bars . . 52
Chocolate Date Energy Bites 55
Chocolate Chip Soft Pretzel Bites 56
Chocolate Kettle Corn 58
Dark Chocolate Cinnamon Muddy Buddies 60
Circus Animal Snack Mix 62
Chocolate Pretzel GORP 63
Strawberry Dip with Chocolate Bear
   Dunkers 64
Strawberry Hazelnut Quesadillas 65
Chocolate Elvis Sandwiches 67
Cocoa Sugar Tortilla Chips 68
Mini Strawberry "Pizza" Bagels 71
Chocolate & Granola Apple Nachos 72

DESSERTS 75
Chocolate Chip Cookies 76
Double Chocolate Chip Cookies 78
Oatmeal Chocolate Chip Cookies 81
Frosted Red Velvet Cookies 82
Fudgy Dark Chocolate Brownies 84
Fudgy Caramel Brownies 87
Caramel Seven Layer Bars 88
Strawberry Frosted Chocolate Cereal
   Treats 90
S'mores Cheesecake Bars 93
Dark Chocolate Raspberry Truffles 94
Peppermint Hot Chocolate Truffles 96
Mini White Chocolate Berry Lemon
   Parfaits 98
Strawberry & Chocolate Whipped Cream
   Crêpes 101
Chocolate Pudding Pie 102
Dark Chocolate Strawberry Crumble . . . 105
Mocha Ice Cream Float 107
Sugar Cookie Chocolate Ice Cream
   Sandwiches 108
Mini Dark Chocolate Lava Cakes 111
Chocolate Strawberry Shortcakes 112
Dark Chocolate Cupcakes 114
Dark Chocolate Frosted Vanilla
   Cupcakes 117
Coconut Cake with Dark Chocolate
   Frosting 118
Dark Chocolate Drizzled Coffee Bundt
   Cake 120
Peanut Butter Cup Cheesecake 122

Substitutions and Nutrition Clarifications . 124
Acknowledgements 129
About the Author 130

INTRODUCTION

During my freshman year of high school, my Uncle Pat, one of my dad's college buddies, took a yearlong sabbatical from his professorship at a university in Utah. At least once a month, he traveled west to visit our family in California for a few days. During his short vacations, Uncle Pat spent hours running nearly 30 miles around town before showering and preparing dinner for us.

Even as a bachelor, Uncle Pat still loved to cook, so he created elaborate yet healthy meals for us with ingredients of fresh vegetables, grilled chicken, and hearty quinoa. He even cooked brunch one Sunday, where my mom fell in love with his simple two-ingredient banana pancakes.

As a sweet treat to end dinner on his first visit, he surprised us with a five-pound bar of 72% dark chocolate from Trader Joe's®. Between my parents and me, that gigantic block of chocolate disappeared embarrassingly fast. Somehow, only a few squares remained by the time we dropped Uncle Pat off at the airport after his weekend trip. Knowing its popularity, he treated us to another five-pound bar on his next visit... And two on the trip after to ensure we still had a full bar in the pantry after he left!

And thus began my life as a chocoholic.

From then on, Mom always stocked the pantry shelves with eight to ten different types of dark chocolate that varied in size, percentage, and brand. When I arrived home from school, I usually broke off a small piece to savor after my granola bar snack, and I always stopped by the pantry again after dinner for another square or two.

Those habits followed me to college, even though that town lacked a Trader Joe's® and its regular grocery stores offered very limited options. My chocolate love continued throughout my organic chemistry job and grew even more entrenched when I left to blog full-time. In addition to lunch and dinner, I began nibbling on a small piece after breakfast too—and nearly every other time I walked into the kitchen.

So when presented with the opportunity to publish a cookbook, I already knew what the theme would be. Within these pages, you'll find some of my most favorite chocolate dessert recipes, ranging from cookies (P.78) and cupcakes (P.114) to brownies (P.84) and bars (P.88). I also dedicated entire chapters to breakfasts and snacks that curb those sneaky morning and afternoon chocolate cravings. And true to this cookbook's name, all of these recipes are healthier and lower in calories than traditional versions, so you can have your chocolate (cake) and eat it too!

So from one chocolate lover to another, I really hope you enjoy the treats that you try. If you remember to take a picture before eating every last bite, share it on social media and tag #healthierchocolatetreats. I'd love to see what you made!

INGREDIENTS

I practically consider grocery stores my home away from home because I stop by multiple times every week to wander around the aisles and pick up ingredients for creating new recipes. As much as I enjoy grocery shopping, I dislike driving to numerous different stores to hunt down unfamiliar or exotic products, so the majority of the ingredients in these recipes can all be found at standard supermarkets. The most common things you'll need are listed below.

FLOUR. I used a few different types of flour in these recipes: all-purpose, whole wheat, whole wheat pastry, and white whole wheat. Most of these can be found at a regular supermarket, although it's sometimes easier to find both whole wheat pastry flour and white whole wheat flour at a health-oriented grocery store. These latter two flours are lighter in taste and texture than regular whole wheat flour but still have the same health benefits, making them ideal for baked goods that require a tender texture.

GLUTEN-FREE FLOUR. Most individual gluten-free flours lack the same taste or texture as all-purpose flour, so I combine multiple varieties to better simulate wheat-based flour. I list my preferred gluten-free flour blend for each recipe (if applicable) in the Substitutions Appendix (P.124), and all of these include xanthan gum. Xanthan gum is crucial; it imitates gluten's structural properties. Most health-oriented grocery stores will carry it. In many of these recipes, store-bought gluten-free flour blends will work as well.

OATS. Recipes in this cookbook call for both old-fashioned (rolled) oats and instant (quick-cook or minute) oats. If you only stock one canister in your pantry, go with the old-fashioned variety! To make your own instant oats, add the same amount of old-fashioned oats to a food processor, and pulse 7-10 times or until the oats are about half of their original size. Remember to buy certified gluten-free oats for gluten-free recipes!

SOLID SWEETENERS. I used a variety of sweeteners in these recipes. The solid sweeteners you'll need are granulated sugar, light brown sugar, and coconut sugar. The latter two may be substituted for one another since they have similar flavors and are both moister than granulated sugar.

LIQUID SWEETENERS. These recipes use honey, agave, and pure maple syrup as the liquid sweeteners. Both Grade A or B maple syrup will work, but remember to buy the good stuff! The only ingredient on the label should be "maple syrup." I don't recommend substituting faux, pancake, or sugar-free syrups; these will affect both the taste and texture of the finished baked good. If you don't have any of these liquid sweeteners, substitute ½ cup of light brown sugar plus ¼ cup of milk for every ½ cup of liquid sweetener.

FATS. I prefer unsalted butter and coconut oil for baking. In general, they're interchangeable, although I definitely recommend sticking with butter for the Chocolate Chip Cookies (P.76), Double Chocolate Chip Cookies (P.78), and Frosted Red Velvet Cookies (P.82)! Butter gives each of these cookies their irreplaceable rich flavor. If you prefer salted butter, adjust the amount of salt in the corresponding recipe accordingly.

EGGS. All of these recipes were tested with large eggs. The brand or color doesn't matter, only the size! All eggs should be at room temperature for two reasons: (a) cold eggs will rapidly chill and re-solidify the fat into tiny blobs, and (b) the emulsifiers in the egg yolk perform better at room temperature. If you're like me and usually forget to set out your eggs ahead of time, here's a little trick! Microwave 1 cup of water for 20-25 seconds; then set your eggs inside for about 5 minutes while measuring the dry ingredients. By the time you're ready to add the eggs to the bowl, they'll be at room temperature!

MILK AND BUTTERMILK. These recipes were tested with nonfat, light soy, and unsweetened cashew milk. Except for the Chocolate Chip Buttermilk Pancakes (P.24) and Chocolate Pudding Pie (P.102), any milk will work. Use whatever you normally keep on hand! Since I rarely finish off a carton of buttermilk, I highly recommend powdered buttermilk made by either Bob's Red Mill® or Saco®. (The latter can be found at many regular grocery stores, including Walmart®!) Powdered buttermilk is shelf-stable and will keep for months in the refrigerator, so you can simply use what you need. Alternatively, add 1 tablespoon of vinegar into a measuring cup, and add enough milk of your choice to reach the 1-cup mark.

GREEK YOGURT. If you read my blog, you'll know that Greek yogurt is my favorite ingredient for healthier baking. It adds the same moisture as excess butter or oil for a fraction of the calories, and it provides a protein boost too! I always use plain nonfat Greek yogurt, and I buy the large tubs at the grocery store. Any brand will work.

VANILLA EXTRACT. All of these recipes were tested with pure vanilla extract. Use the best vanilla you can afford, and you'll really notice the flavor difference, especially in the Chocolate Chip Cookies (P.76)!

COCOA POWDER. I went through lots of cocoa powder writing this cookbook! All of these recipes were tested with Hershey's® unsweetened cocoa powder. If you prefer their dark (Dutched) variety, you're welcome to substitute that instead.

CHOCOLATE CHIPS. These recipes use both regular-sized and miniature chocolate chips. Any brand will work. I generally prefer (a) Hershey's for dark chocolate chips because they're the same size as traditional semisweet chips, whereas many other brands are much larger; (b) Ghirardelli for semisweet, miniature, and white chocolate chips; and (c) EnjoyLife for vegan chocolate chips.

COOKING SPRAY. Many of these recipes use cooking spray to grease the baking pans. It's much easier than doing it by hand, especially for the Dark Chocolate Cupcakes (P.114) and Vanilla Cupcakes (P.117)! Any type (canola, coconut, etc.) will generally work. However, the Coffee Bundt Cake (P.120) requires cooking spray with flour, also called baking spray, because the cake tends to stick to the ruffled edges of the bundt cake pan with regular cooking spray.

RECIPE INGREDIENTS GUIDE. Underneath many recipes, you'll find one or more of the following symbols that indicate whether the recipe adheres to particular dietary restrictions.

C	clean eating	DF	dairy-free
GF	gluten-free	HP	high protein
V	vegan	P	paleo

MEASUREMENTS

While a pinch of this or a handful of that may work in cooking, baking requires quite a bit more precision! To ensure your treats turn out properly, it's important to measure all of the ingredients correctly. I highly recommend purchasing a kitchen scale, especially for measuring dry ingredients. They're fairly inexpensive, as little as $15, and worth their weight in gold. Kitchen scales ensure your baked goods turn out consistently and perfect every time. I use my kitchen scale for every recipe I make! The best measuring practices for the most common ingredients are below.

FLOUR, OATS AND COCOA POWDER. These dry ingredients should be measured using either a kitchen scale or the spoon-and-level method. For the latter, scoop the dry ingredient from the container using a regular spoon, and lightly transfer it into the measuring cup. I often shake the spoon back and forth to do so. Continue adding the dry ingredient to the measuring cup in this manner until the cup is overflowing; then scrape the flat backside of a knife across the top of the measuring cup to level.

SOLID SWEETENERS. These dry ingredients may be measured with a kitchen scale as well. Alternatively, granulated and coconut sugar may be poured directly from the container into the measuring cup. Brown sugar should be gently packed into the measuring cup using the backside of a regular spoon.

LIQUID SWEETENERS. These should be measured using the corresponding measuring cups or spoons. I always scrape out the lingering sweetener stuck to the inside with a spatula.

FATS. Both coconut oil and unsalted butter should be measured when solid and melted afterward. Coconut oil melts around 70°F, so remember to store it in the refrigerator during the hot summer months!

HEALTHIER CHOCOLATE TREATS ♥ 11

EQUIPMENT

Because I began my baking blog while still in college, I had very little storage space in my tiny apartment kitchen. I could barely fit all of my weekly groceries in the cupboards, let alone any baking ingredients! Therefore, nearly all of the recipes on both my blog and in this cookbook can be made with basic baking and kitchen equipment. Everything you will need is included below.

MIXING BOWLS. I recommend two large mixing bowls and two smaller ones. For many of the baking recipes, you'll need to whisk together the dry ingredients (use the smaller bowls) before adding them to the egg mixture (in the larger bowls). Generally, oversized soup bowls will work for the smaller size. If you can, try to find larger bowls that are dishwasher-safe; you'll have fewer things to wash by hand!

MEASURING CUPS AND SPOONS. One set of each will suffice, although sometimes a second set comes in handy, like when you just used your teaspoon for vanilla and forgot to add a teaspoon of cinnamon to the other bowl. (I've done that too many times to count!)

KITCHEN SCALE. This is optional but really nice to have, especially for measuring dry ingredients. They're fairly inexpensive, starting around $15, and ensure that your baked goods turn out perfectly every time. I use mine for every recipe that I make.

SHARP KNIVES. For slicing ingredients and baked goods, I generally use a 3½" paring knife or 6" chef's knife. Use whatever you feel most comfortable with.

WHISK. In many recipes, the dry ingredients should be whisked together. Whisking ensures more even mixing than a spoon or fork, and it also breaks up any lingering flour clumps.

ROLLING PIN. I absolutely adore my silicone rolling pin, but an old-fashioned wooden one will work just fine to roll out the Sugar Cookies (P.108) for ice cream sandwiches. If you don't have either, try using a tall thin bottle instead.

ROUND COOKIE CUTTERS. For the Sugar Cookie Chocolate Ice Cream Sandwiches (P.108), I cut out the cookies with a 2 ½"-round biscuit cutter. Round cutters work best for assembling the ice cream sandwiches, but cute shapes would be fun too!

HAND-HELD ELECTRIC MIXER. An electric mixer comes in really handy for a few of the recipes, including the Peanut Butter Cup Cheesecake (P.122), S'mores Cheesecake Bars (P.93), and Chocolate Yogurt Frosting (P.114). The hand-held version is compact and relatively inexpensive, and that is what I use most often. However, a more expensive stand mixer would work, too.

WIRE COOLING RACKS. I recommend at least one large or two smaller cooling racks. Transferring warm baked goods from their pans to the cooling racks ensures that their bottoms don't burn or turn soggy, and it also helps them cool faster.

BAKING SHEETS. I prefer rimless, light-colored aluminum baking sheets, especially the type labeled "air" or "air baking sheet" with an extra layer of metal on the bottom. Darker baking sheets are prone to burning the bottoms of baked goods, and ones with a rim sometimes burn the edges of baked goods closest to the outside of the pan. I own three sizes (9"x14", 12"x14", and 14"x16"), but if you only have space for one, buy the largest size.

SILICONE BAKING MATS. I love these! They're reusable and dishwasher-safe, and they store quite easily. Parchment paper may be substituted, if you prefer.

BAKING PANS. These recipes require a few different sizes of baking pans. It's very important to use the exact pan specified by the recipe; substituting a different one often yields subpar baked goods. You'll need the following:
- one 8"-square
- one 9"-square
- two 9" rounds
- one 9" springform
- one 12-cup bundt

STANDARD SIZE MUFFIN PAN. While traditional metal muffin pans work well, I adore my silicone muffin pans. Metal pans often brown the bottoms of the muffins more than the tops, but silicone pans only turn the bottoms a shade or two darker than those golden tops. The baking times will remain the same regardless of which version you use.

9" PIE PLATE. This is for the Chocolate Pudding Pie (P.102), and deeper pie plates work better for this recipe. People rarely turn down extra filling!

LARGE COOKING POT WITH LID. The Chocolate Kettle Corn (P.58) is cooked in a large pot on the stove. I prefer darker nonstick pots with glass lids for making popcorn so you can see when the kernels finish popping.

LARGE PAN. To cook the Chocolate Chip Buttermilk Pancakes (P.24) and Banana French Toast (P.27), I use a 10" skillet. If you prefer an electric griddle, that works fine too.

HIGH-SPEED BLENDER. These powerful blenders make mixing up smoothies and frappuccinos look easy! I currently own and love my Ninja® blender. Vitamix® and Blendtec® are more expensive options.

FOOD PROCESSOR. I use a food processor for making graham cracker crusts. However, a blender will work just fine too.

CULINARY TORCH. A culinary torch comes in handy for toasting marshmallows for the S'mores Cheesecake Bars (P.93). A long-nosed lighter can be used instead.

ICE CREAM SCOOP. To make the scoops of ice cream in the Sugar Cookie Chocolate Ice Cream Sandwiches (P.108) look pretty and round, use an ice cream scoop. Since a regular spoon will work as well, this is optional.

PARFAIT OR WINE GLASSES. For an elegant presentation of the White Chocolate Berry Lemon Parfaits (P.98), I like to use small parfait or wine glasses. However, these are entirely optional.

BREAKFASTS

♥ ♥ ♥

Even as a little girl, I've always been a morning person. Back then, I rose before the sun and sprang out of bed, full of energy and excitement for the play dates and sports practices that lay ahead. Although I may need a few more moments snuggled in between the sheets these days, I still look forward to the calmness and promise of the quiet morning hours—especially when one of these breakfast treats is waiting for me!

STRAWBERRY BANANA CHOCOLATE CHIP MUFFINS

prep time: 25 minutes ♥ baking time: 24-27 minutes ♥ yields: 12 muffins

A few times each year, my mom bought extra bananas during her mid-week grocery shopping trip, and she would pull out the well-worn, yellowing recipe card from her collection the following weekend to bake banana muffins. She usually left hers plain, but I couldn't resist creating a healthier recipe with a few extra goodies mixed in!

- 1 ¾ cups (210g) white whole wheat flour
- ¾ tsp baking powder
- ¾ tsp baking soda
- ¼ tsp salt
- 1 tbsp (14g) unsalted butter, melted and cooled slightly
- 1 large egg, room temperature
- 1 ½ tsp vanilla extract
- ½ cup (105g) mashed banana (about 1 medium)
- ¼ cup (60g) plain nonfat Greek yogurt
- ⅓ cup (80mL) pure maple syrup
- 3 tbsp (45mL) nonfat milk
- 1 ½ cups (210g) frozen unsweetened strawberries, thawed slightly and diced
- 2 tbsp (28g) miniature chocolate chips

1. Preheat the oven to 350°F, and lightly coat 12 muffins cups with nonstick cooking spray.
2. Whisk together the flour, baking powder, baking soda, and salt in a medium bowl. In a separate bowl, whisk together the butter, egg, and vanilla. Mix in the mashed banana and Greek yogurt, stirring until no large lumps remain. Stir in the maple syrup. Alternate between adding the flour mixture and the milk to the egg mixture, beginning and ending with the flour mixture, and stirring until just incorporated. (For best results, add the flour mixture in 3 equal parts.) Gently fold in the strawberries and 1 ½ tablespoons of miniature chocolate chips.
3. Divide the batter between the prepared muffin cups, and press the remaining miniature chocolate chips into the tops. Bake at 350°F for 24-27 minutes or until a toothpick inserted into the center comes out clean. Cool the muffins in the muffin cups for 5 minutes before carefully transferring them to a wire rack.

AMY'S ADVICE
Try fresh strawberries or blueberries when they're in season!

Nutrition Information: 128 calories | 2.4g fat (1.1g saturated fat, 0.6g unsaturated fat) | 18.2mg cholesterol | 168.7mg sodium | 24.5g carbohydrates (2.7g fiber, 8.9g sugar) | 3.7g protein

DOUBLE CHOCOLATE ZUCCHINI MUFFINS

prep time: 20 minutes ♥ baking time: 24-26 minutes ♥ yields: 9 muffins

Throughout my childhood, my grandma would fly out from Ohio once a year to visit, and she always packed two loaves of freshly baked zucchini bread in her suitcase. Although not the biggest fan of vegetables back then, I could easily polish off an entire loaf by myself! These muffins are a healthier version of her irresistible recipe, with lots of extra chocolate added in too.

1 cup (120g) white whole wheat flour
¾ cup (60g) unsweetened cocoa powder
2 tsp baking powder
¼ tsp salt
1 tbsp (14g) unsalted butter, melted and cooled slightly
1 large egg, room temperature
1 large egg white, room temperature
1 tsp vanilla extract
¼ cup (60g) plain nonfat Greek yogurt
½ cup (120mL) pure maple syrup
¼ cup (60mL) nonfat milk
1 cup (110g) shredded zucchini
2 tbsp (28g) miniature chocolate chips

1. Preheat the oven to 350°F, and lightly coat 9 muffin cups with nonstick cooking spray.

2. Whisk together the flour, cocoa powder, baking powder, and salt in a medium bowl. In a separate bowl, whisk together the butter, egg, egg white, and vanilla. Stir in the Greek yogurt, mixing until no large lumps remain. Stir in the maple syrup. Alternate between adding the flour mixture and the milk to the egg mixture, beginning and ending with the flour mixture, and stirring until just incorporated. (For best results, add the flour mixture in 3 equal parts.) Gently fold in the zucchini and 1 ½ tablespoons of miniature chocolate chips.

3. Divide the batter between the prepared muffin cups, and gently press the remaining miniature chocolate chips into the tops. Bake at 350°F for 24-26 minutes or until the centers feel firm. Cool the muffins in the muffin cups for 5 minutes before carefully transferring them to a wire rack.

AMY'S ADVICE
I love reheating leftover muffins in the microwave for 12-15 seconds to make the chocolate chips melt!

Nutrition Information: 152 calories | 3.7g fat (1.5g saturated fat, 0.8g unsaturated fat) | 24.3mg cholesterol 281.6mg sodium | 29.2g carbohydrates (4.5g fiber, 13.3g sugar) | 5.2g protein

DARK CHOCOLATE DRIZZLED BLUEBERRY SCONES

prep time: 15 minutes ♥ baking time: 15-18 minutes ♥ yields: 8 scones

I ate my first scone while on vacation with my dad in Seattle at our upscale hotel's dining room. Soft on the inside, crisp on the outside, and buttery throughout, the scone was a little bite of bliss on that dreary morning! I waited more than seven years to bake my own at home, but every time I do, I think about our trip and those perfect Seattle scones.

for the scones
- 1 ½ cups (180g) whole wheat flour
- 1 ½ tsp baking powder
- ¼ tsp salt
- 2 tbsp (28g) unsalted butter, cold and cubed
- ½ cup (120g) plain nonfat Greek yogurt
- 3 tbsp + 2 tsp (55mL) nonfat milk, divided
- 2 tbsp (30mL) agave
- 2 tsp vanilla extract
- ¼ cup (40g) dried wild blueberries

for the drizzle
- 2 tbsp (10g) unsweetened cocoa powder
- 1 tsp agave
- 4 tsp nonfat milk

1. Preheat the oven to 425°F, and line a baking sheet with a silicone baking mat or parchment paper.
2. To prepare the scones, whisk together the flour, baking powder, and salt in a medium bowl. Cut in the butter with a pastry cutter or the back of a fork until the mixture resembles fine crumbs. Make a well in the center. Add the Greek yogurt, 3 tablespoons of milk, agave, and vanilla, mixing until just incorporated. Fold in the dried blueberries.
3. Transfer the dough to the prepared baking sheet, and shape into a ¾"-tall circle. Brush the remaining milk over the top and around the sides, and slice the circle into 8 wedges. Bake at 425°F for 15-18 minutes or until light golden brown on top. Cool the scones on the pan for 5 minutes before transferring them to a wire rack.
4. While the scones bake, prepare the drizzle. Mix together the cocoa powder, agave, and milk in a small bowl. Drizzle over the tops of the cooled scones.

AMY'S ADVICE
Try chopped dried cherries for a fun twist!

Nutrition Information: 159 calories | 3.5g fat (1.9g saturated fat, 1.0g unsaturated fat) | 8.0mg cholesterol 191.6mg sodium | 29.8g carbohydrates (3.7g fiber, 10.4g sugar) | 5.2g protein

PUMPKIN CHOCOLATE CHIP SCONES

prep time: 15 minutes ♥ baking time: 12-14 minutes ♥ yields: 8 scones

I first baked these scones while visiting my parents, and I set aside a few of the leftovers for my mom to bring into work to share with one of her friends. That morning, they sent me two pictures. The first captured the sweet lady smiling while holding the plate of scones, and the second arrived five minutes later, showing the same plate with only a few crumbs and chocolate smears left!

1 ½ cups (180g) whole wheat flour
1 ½ tsp baking powder
1 tsp ground cinnamon
¼ tsp salt
2 tbsp (28g) unsalted butter, cold and cubed
½ cup (122g) pumpkin purée
8 tsp maple syrup
3 tbsp (45mL) nonfat milk, divided
2 tbsp (28g) miniature chocolate chips

1. Preheat the oven to 425°F, and line a baking sheet with a silicone baking mat or parchment paper.
2. To prepare the scones, whisk together the flour, baking powder, cinnamon, and salt in a medium bowl. Cut in the butter with a pastry cutter or the back of a fork until the mixture resembles fine crumbs. Make a well in the center. Add the pumpkin purée, maple syrup, and 10 teaspoons of milk, mixing until just incorporated. Fold in the miniature chocolate chips.
3. Divide the dough into 8 equal portions, and shape each into a ball. Place onto the prepared baking sheet, and flatten slightly. Brush the remaining milk over the tops of the scones. Bake at 425°F for 12-14 minutes or until light golden brown on top. Cool the scones on the pan for 5 minutes before transferring to a wire rack.

AMY'S ADVICE
For an extra chocolaty touch, add the dark chocolate drizzle on P.20!

C

Nutrition Information: 145 calories | 4.4g fat (2.4g saturated fat, 1.0g unsaturated fat) | 7.9mg cholesterol 168.2mg sodium | 25.1g carbohydrates (3.5g fiber, 6.8g sugar) | 3.5g protein

CHOCOLATE CHIP BUTTERMILK PANCAKES

prep time: 10 minutes ♥ cooking time: 15-20 minutes ♥ yields: 4 servings

During my senior year of high school, a few of my marching band friends and I started going out to eat after we performed at football games on Friday nights. Because nearly every restaurant in town closed early except for a pancake house, we ended up there, and everyone ordered chocolate chip pancakes. It quickly became our tradition, and to this day, none of us can order "CCPK's" unless the others are present! To stay true to our unspoken promise, I created this healthier recipe to get my CCPK fix at home in between visits.

- 1 ⅛ cup (135g) whole wheat pastry flour
- 1 tsp baking soda
- ½ tsp baking powder
- ¼ tsp salt
- ½ tbsp (7g) unsalted butter, melted and cooled slightly
- 1 large egg, room temperature
- 1 ½ tsp vanilla extract
- ½ cup + 1 tbsp (135mL) low-fat buttermilk, room temperature
- 1 tsp pure maple syrup
- ¼ cup (60g) plain nonfat Greek yogurt
- 1 ½ tbsp (21g) miniature chocolate chips

1. Whisk together the flour, baking soda, baking powder, and salt in a medium bowl. In a separate bowl, whisk together the butter, egg, and vanilla. Whisk in the buttermilk and maple syrup. Mix in the Greek yogurt, stirring until no large lumps remain. Add the flour mixture, and stir until just incorporated. Gently fold in the miniature chocolate chips.
2. Lightly coat a large pan or griddle with nonstick cooking spray, and preheat it over low heat.
3. Using 2 tablespoons of batter for each pancake, dollop it onto the hot pan, and spread the batter into a circular shape. Let the pancakes cook for 2-3 minutes or until a slight skin starts to form around the edges and the bottom is light golden brown. Slide a spatula underneath and flip. Continue to cook the pancakes for another 1-2 minutes or until light golden brown on both sides. Serve hot.

AMY'S ADVICE
This recipe is easily doubled to make more. If you have any leftovers, they freeze really well, too!

C

Nutrition Information: 212 calories | 5.6g fat (2.2g saturated fat, 1.3g unsaturated fat) | 51.8mg cholesterol 581.9mg sodium | 33.0g carbohydrates (4.5g fiber, 6.5g sugar) | 8.7g protein

BANANA FRENCH TOAST WITH CHOCOLATE SYRUP

prep time: 5 minutes ♥ cooking time: 15-20 minutes ♥ yields: 4 servings

During college, my mom and I visited Alaska one summer and stayed at a cute B&B overlooking the ocean. The owner insisted on cooking French toast for us one morning, and after we exclaimed that it was some of the best we had ever tasted, she explained her secret. She always used whole wheat bread with a sprinkle of nutmeg to bring out the bread's nuttiness. I've made my French toast that way

for the syrup
2 tbsp (10g) unsweetened cocoa powder
1 tsp honey
5 tsp nonfat milk

for the french toast
½ cup (105g) mashed banana (about 1 medium)
1 large egg, lightly beaten
¾ cup (180mL) nonfat milk
¼ tsp ground cinnamon
⅛ tsp ground nutmeg
8 slices low-calorie double fiber whole wheat bread

1. Preheat the oven to 200°F, and place two wire racks onto a large rimmed baking sheet.
2. To prepare the chocolate drizzle, stir together the cocoa powder, honey, and milk in a small bowl until smooth.
3. To prepare the French toast, whisk together the banana, egg, milk, cinnamon, and nutmeg in a shallow bowl or pie plate.
4. Coat 2 large pans with nonstick cooking spray, and preheat over medium-low heat. When the pans are hot, dip 1 slice of bread at a time into the egg mixture, lightly coating each side, and place the slice into the hot pan. Cook each slice for 2-3 minutes per side or until golden brown. Transfer the cooked French toast onto the prepared wire racks, and place the baking sheets in the oven to keep the French toast warm. Repeat with the remaining bread and egg mixture. Serve warm, lightly drizzled with the chocolate syrup.

AMY'S ADVICE
Serve this French toast with fresh fruit for an easy weekend brunch!

Nutrition Information: 181 calories | 2.6g fat (0.5g saturated fat, 0.8g unsaturated fat) | 47.6mg cholesterol 342.9mg sodium | 40.7g carbohydrates (11.8g fiber, 12.3g sugar) | 10.2g protein

STRAWBERRY & DARK CHOCOLATE SWEET ROLLS

prep time: 35 minutes ♥ inactive time: 15 minutes
baking time: 30-35 minutes ♥ yields: 12 sweet rolls

A few times each year, my family visits the local country club to enjoy their gourmet buffet-style brunch. Servers set up two long tables overflowing with traditional sweet and savory dishes, a separate carving station with omelettes made to order, and a final table filled with desserts. The sweet treats always include chocolate-covered strawberries, and those were the inspiration for these healthier breakfast rolls.

for the rolls
½ cup (120mL) warm unsweetened cashew milk (100-110°F)
6 tbsp (90mL) agave
1 tsp coconut oil, melted
1 tsp vanilla extract
¼ tsp salt
2 ¼ tsp (one ¼ oz envelope) yeast
2 ¼ – 3 ½ cups (270-420g) whole wheat flour
2 ½ cups (210g) frozen unsweetened strawberries, thawed slightly
1 tbsp (8g) cornstarch
small bowl of water

for the drizzle
3 tbsp (15g) unsweetened cocoa powder
1 tbsp (15mL) agave
5 tsp unsweetened cashew milk

1. Lightly coat a 9"-round cake pan with nonstick cooking spray.
2. Stir together the warm cashew milk, agave, coconut oil, vanilla, salt, and yeast in a large bowl. Add 1 ¾ cups of flour, and stir until it's completely incorporated. Continue adding flour, 2-3 tablespoons at a time, until the dough no longer sticks to the sides of the bowl. Turn the dough out onto a clean well-floured surface, and knead for a few minutes or until it springs back when you gently press your index finger into it. Let the dough rest for at least 10 minutes.
3. While waiting, prepare the filling. Dice the strawberries, and toss them with the cornstarch in a medium bowl until they're evenly coated.
4. Re-flour the work surface if necessary, and lightly flour a rolling pin. Roll out the dough into a 12"x16" rectangle. Spread the strawberries into a single layer on top of the dough, leaving a 1" border on the two longer edges. Starting at one longer edge, carefully roll up the dough into a log towards the opposite longer edge, trying not the squash the strawberries too much. Brush water onto the second longer edge where it meets the dough log before pinching the dough shut to seal.

C V

Nutrition Information: 152 calories | 3.7g fat (1.5g saturated fat, 0.8g unsaturated fat) | 24.3mg cholesterol 281.6mg sodium | 29.2g carbohydrates (4.5g fiber, 13.3g sugar) | 5.2g protein

5. Slice the dough log into 12 equal portions using dental floss or a sharp serrated knife. Place them cut side down into the prepared pan.
6. Preheat the oven to 350°F while letting the rolls rest in the pan. Bake at 350°F for 32-35 minutes or until the spirals of the rolls in the center feel mostly firm. Cool in the pan for at least 5 minutes before removing.
7. To prepare the drizzle, stir together the cocoa powder, agave, and cashew milk in a small bowl. Drizzle on top of the rolls just before serving.

CHOCOLATE FUDGE BROWNIE OATMEAL

prep time: 3 minutes ♥ cooking time: 2 minutes ♥ yields: 1 serving

During a few quarters of college, I enrolled in early morning classes with lectures that began shortly after the sun started peeking over the horizon. Before biking to campus in the freezing cold fog, I'd bribe myself to get out of bed with a bowl of rich, chocolaty oatmeal. With a few chocolate chips sprinkled on top, it did the trick every time!

⅓ cup (33g) old-fashioned oats
⅔ cup (160mL) nonfat milk
2 tbsp (10g) unsweetened cocoa powder
1 tsp Truvia®

1. Add the oats, milk, cocoa powder, and Truvia® to a microwave-safe bowl, and stir until thoroughly combined. Microwave the bowl on HIGH for 2 minutes 15 seconds, stirring every 45 seconds, or until the oatmeal has thickened. Let the oatmeal cool for 2 minutes before eating.

AMY'S ADVICE
For cold overnight oats, add all of the ingredients to a mason jar, and refrigerate overnight or for at least 8 hours.

C

Nutrition Information: 175 calories | 3.1g fat (0.1g saturated fat, 1.4g unsaturated fat) | 3.3mg cholesterol 198.7mg sodium | 32.1g carbohydrates (6.7g fiber, 9.0g sugar) | 10.9g protein

WHITE CHOCOLATE BERRY CHEESECAKE OATMEAL

prep time: 3 minutes ♥ cooking time: 2 minutes ♥ yields: 1 serving

My family went camping twice each summer throughout my childhood, and every morning, Mom would heat up water on our old gas-powered stove to make hot chocolate and instant oatmeal. That was the only time we ate oatmeal, so I didn't realize it was possible to make my own from scratch until I reached high school. This fun version tastes much better, and it even comes with fresh fruit!

⅓ cup (33g) old-fashioned oats
⅔ cup (160mL) nonfat milk
1 serving (7g) sugar-free, fat-free instant cheesecake pudding mix
½ tbsp (7g) chopped white chocolate
¼ cup (35g) fresh raspberries, diced

1. Add the oats, milk, and pudding mix to a microwave-safe bowl, and stir until thoroughly combined. Microwave the bowl on HIGH for 2 minutes 15 seconds, stirring every 45 seconds, or until the oatmeal has thickened.

2. Immediately add the white chocolate, stirring until it has melted. Stir in the raspberries. Let the oatmeal cool for 2 minutes before eating.

AMY'S ADVICE
Try blueberries, strawberries, or even blackberries instead!

Nutrition Information: 207 calories | 3.2g fat (0.6g saturated fat, 1.5g unsaturated fat) | 3.8mg cholesterol 380.7mg sodium | 35.9g carbohydrates (4.9g fiber, 9.0g sugar) | 9.3g protein

DARK CHOCOLATE CHERRY GRANOLA

prep time: 5 minutes ♥ baking time: 40-45 minutes ♥ yields: 8 servings

My junior year of college, I started baking homemade granola every Saturday to snack on throughout the week. During one baking session, I decided to make a double batch to save a little time the following weekend. But by Friday night, my granola jar was completely empty! I proclaimed myself a granola addict that evening, and it's been true ever since.

1 ½ cups (150g) old-fashioned oats
2 cups (60g) crisp brown rice cereal
2 tbsp (10g) unsweetened cocoa powder
1 tsp coconut oil, melted
¼ cup (60mL) warm water
3 tbsp (45mL) agave
1 large egg white, room temperature
⅓ cup (53g) dried cherries

1. Preheat the oven to 350°F, and lightly coat a 9"-square baking pan with nonstick cooking spray.
2. Stir together the oats, rice cereal, and cocoa powder in a large bowl. In a separate bowl, whisk together the coconut oil, water, agave, and egg white. Pour the water mixture into the cereal mixture, stirring with a spatula until all of the cereal is coated.
3. Spread the cereal mixture into the prepared pan. Bake at 350°F for 40-45 minutes or until crunchy, gently stirring every 15 minutes to break up the clusters and move them around the pan. Cool the granola completely in the pan before sprinkling the dried cherries on top.

C

Nutrition Information: 133 calories | 1.9g fat (0.5g saturated fat, 0.8g unsaturated fat) | 0.0mg cholesterol
64.4mg sodium | 21.2g carbohydrates (2.3g fiber, 9.4g sugar) | 3.2g protein

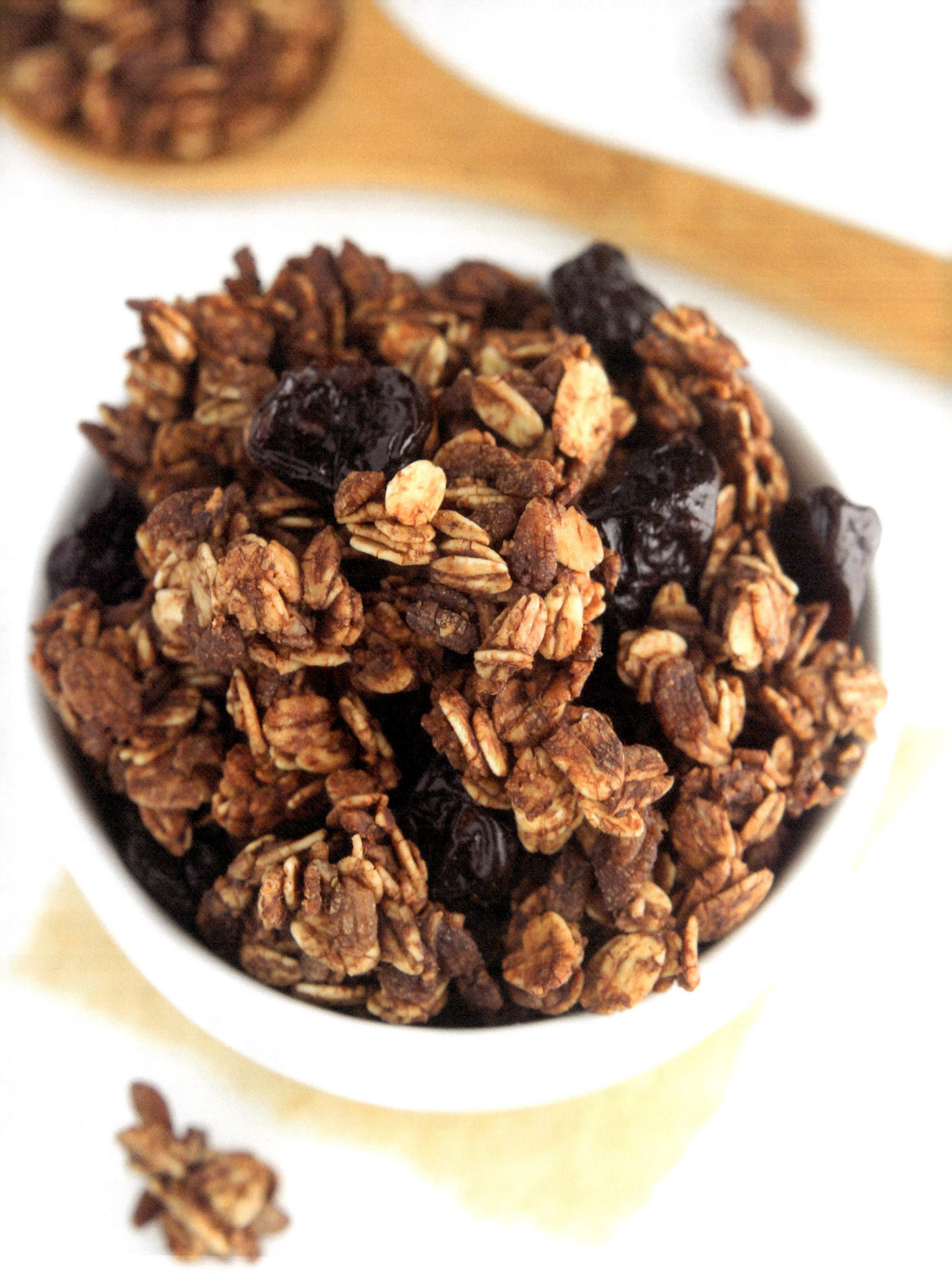

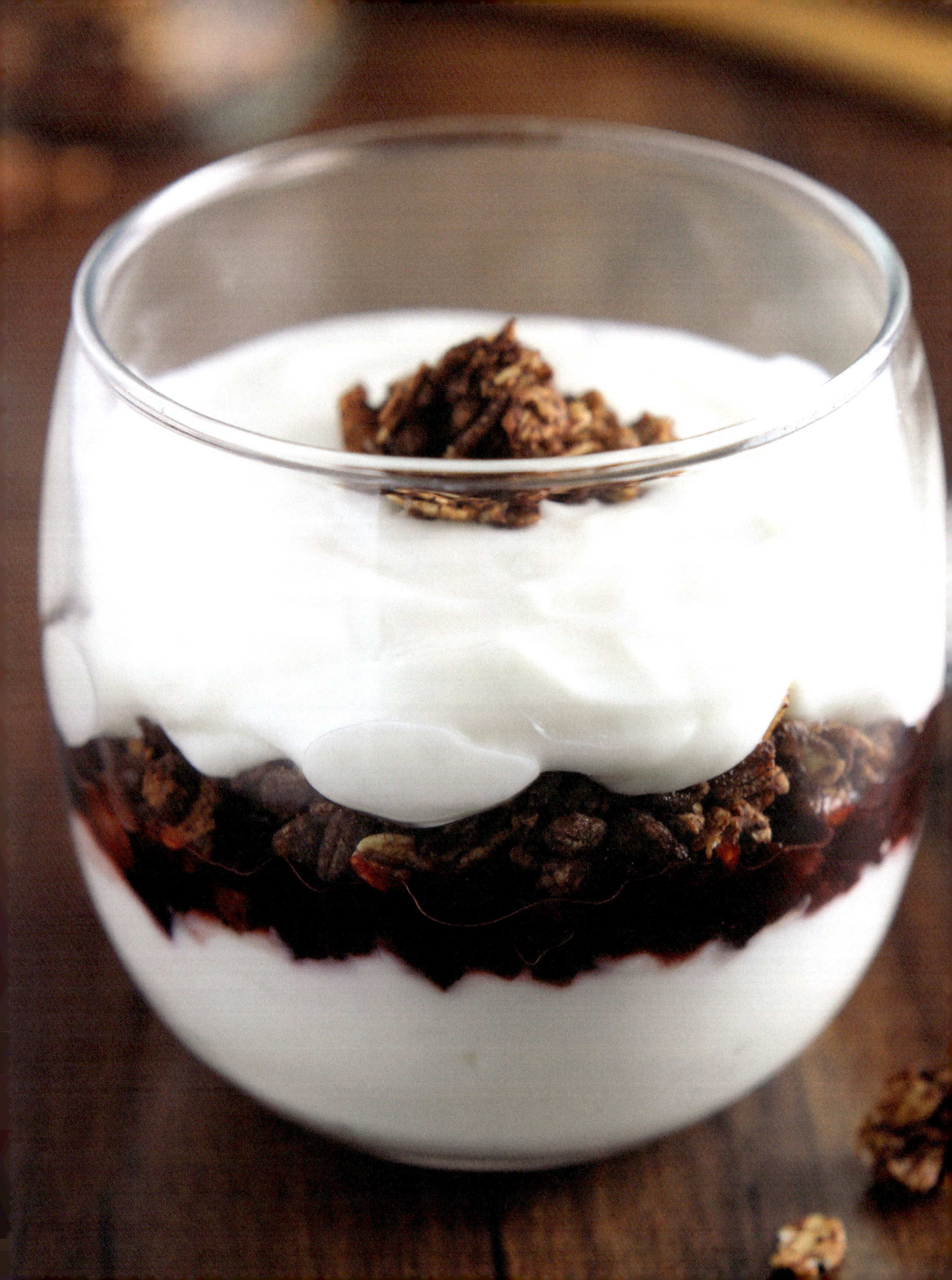

DARK CHOCOLATE CHERRY YOGURT PARFAITS

prep time: 5 minutes ♥ yields: 2 parfaits

I lived in the dorms during my freshman year of college and ate most of my meals in the dining hall. On certain nights when most of the entrées were unrecognizable, I filled a bowl with yogurt from the salad bar and topped it with crunchy granola from the cereal bins. Paired with a side of salad or fresh fruit, I always enjoyed those healthier breakfast-for-dinner options!

1 ½ cups (360g) plain nonfat Greek yogurt
4 tsp Truvia®
1 ½ cups (210g) fresh pitted cherries, diced
½ cup (75g) Dark Chocolate Cherry Granola (P.34)

1. Stir together the Greek yogurt and Truvia® in a medium bowl.
2. Add a scant ½ cup of the sweetened yogurt to each of two parfait glasses. Sprinkle a scant ½ cup of cherries and 3 tablespoons of granola on top. Add the remaining yogurt to the parfait glasses, and top with the remaining cherries and granola.

AMY'S ADVICE
For a quick shortcut, substitute vanilla nonfat Greek yogurt instead of the plain nonfat Greek yogurt and Truvia®.

C   HP

Nutrition Information: 305 calories | 2.1g fat (0.5g saturated fat, 0.9g unsaturated fat) | 0.0mg cholesterol 143.2mg sodium | 44.8g carbohydrates (5.5g fiber, 29.6g sugar) | 21.6g protein

WHITE CHOCOLATE CINNAMON APPLE COFFEE CAKE

prep time: 20 minutes ♥ baking time: 40-50 minutes ♥ yields: 9 slices

My family's favorite brunch restaurant is famous for their blueberry coffee cake: tall slices of white sour cream cake full of juicy berries and topped with a thick cinnamon streusel. While they sell their classic version all year round, they also offer seasonal flavors throughout the year. As purists, we rarely try the others, but when the waiter sent us home with an apple-themed slice on the house one fall, I quickly decided to recreate a healthier version after my first bite—with a little chocolate spin, of course!

for the topping
- ½ cup (60g) whole wheat flour
- 1 tsp ground cinnamon
- 1 tbsp (14g) unsalted butter, melted and cooled slightly
- 2 tbsp (30mL) maple syrup

for the cake
- 1 ¾ cups (210g) whole wheat flour
- 2 tsp ground cinnamon
- 1 ½ tsp baking powder
- ½ tsp baking soda
- ¼ tsp salt
- 1 tbsp (14g) unsalted butter, melted and cooled slightly
- 1 large egg, room temperature
- 2 tsp vanilla extract
- ½ cup (120g) plain nonfat Greek yogurt
- ⅓ cup (80mL) maple syrup
- 6 tbsp (90mL) nonfat milk
- 1 cup (135g) diced red apple (about 1 medium)
- ¼ cup (56g) white chocolate chips, chopped

1. Preheat the oven to 350°F, and lightly coat an 8"-square pan with nonstick cooking spray.
2. To prepare the topping, whisk together the flour and cinnamon. Thoroughly mix in the butter and maple syrup.
3. To prepare the cake, whisk together the flour, cinnamon, baking powder, baking soda, and salt in a medium bowl. In a separate bowl, whisk together the butter, egg, and vanilla. Mix in the Greek yogurt, stirring until no large lumps remain. Stir in the maple syrup. Alternate between adding the flour mixture and the milk to the egg mixture, beginning and ending with the flour mixture, and stirring until just incorporated. (For best results, add the flour mixture in 3 equal parts.) Gently fold in the apples and white chocolate.
4. Spread the batter into the prepared pan, and evenly sprinkle the crumb topping over the batter. Bake at 350°F for 40-50 minutes or until a toothpick inserted into the center comes out clean. Cool in the pan for at least 10 minutes before slicing and serving.

AMY'S ADVICE
The crumb topping tends to clump, so try to break it up into small chocolate chip-sized pieces.

Nutrition Information: 209 calories | 4.5g fat (2.4g saturated fat, 1.2g unsaturated fat) | 28.2mg cholesterol 237.7mg sodium | 37.1g carbohydrates (4.5g fiber, 12.3g sugar) | 6.6g protein

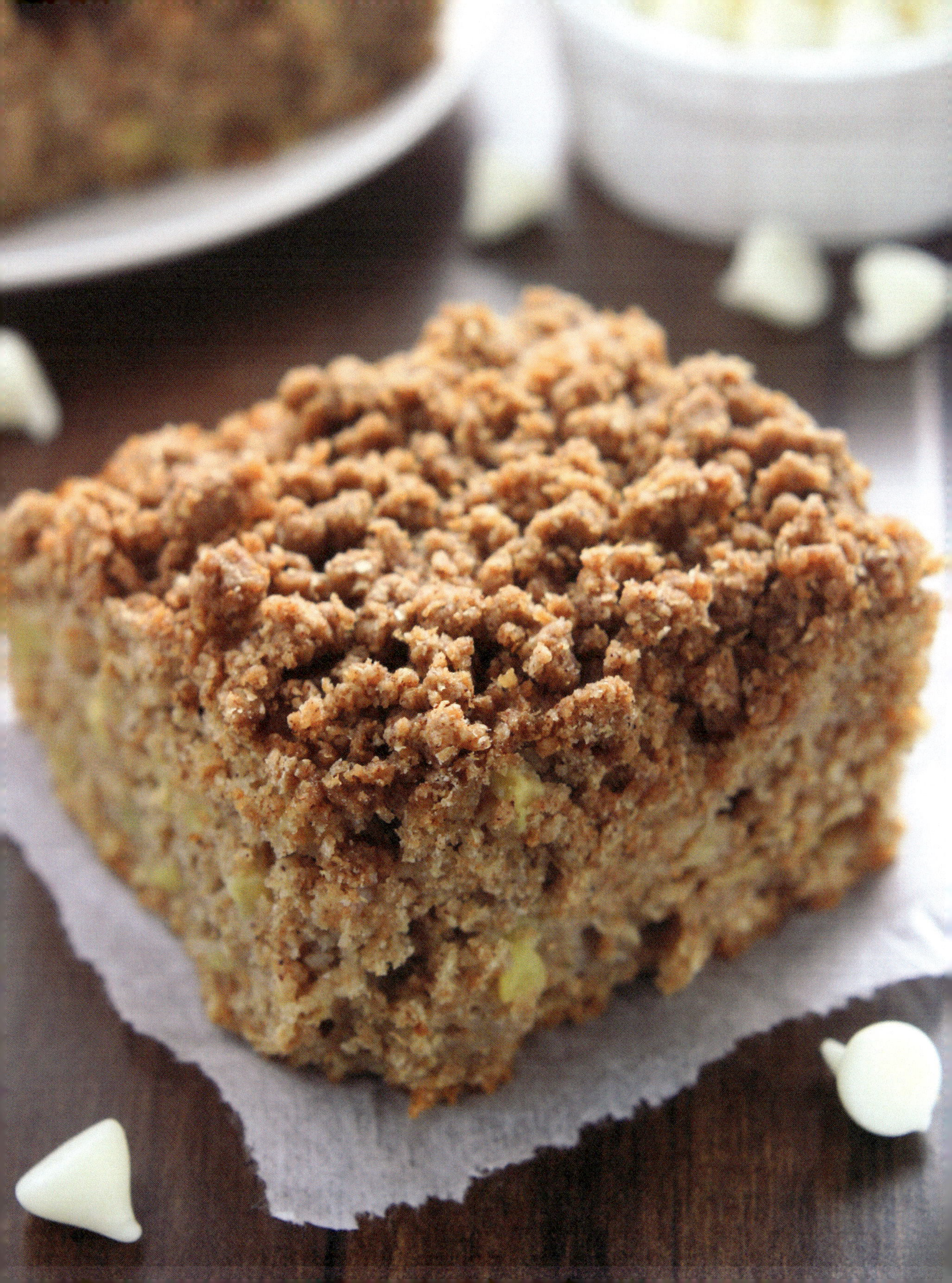

CHOCOLATE COVERED STRAWBERRY GREEN SMOOTHIE

prep time: 5 minutes ♥ yields: 1 smoothie

When I attended my first food blogging conference, I listened to a presentation where one lady described how she and a friend set up a website dedicated entirely to green smoothies. Ironically enough, I had never actually drank one! The week after I returned home, I pulled out my blender and began trying different flavor combinations. I soon discovered how much I love adding cocoa powder because it almost makes the smoothie taste like dessert!

1 cup (140g) frozen unsweetened strawberries
1 cup (240mL) nonfat milk
2 tbsp (10g) unsweetened cocoa powder
1 ½ tsp (7g) Truvia®, or to taste
1 cup (45g) packed baby spinach

1. Add all of the ingredients to a blender in the order listed, and blend until smooth.

AMY'S ADVICE
Try frozen blueberries or raspberries for a fun twist!

C   GF

Nutrition Information: 164 calories | 1.4g fat (0.1g saturated fat, 0.2g unsaturated fat) | 5.0mg cholesterol 267.5mg sodium | 33.2g carbohydrates (8.0g fiber, 19.8g sugar) | 11.9g protein

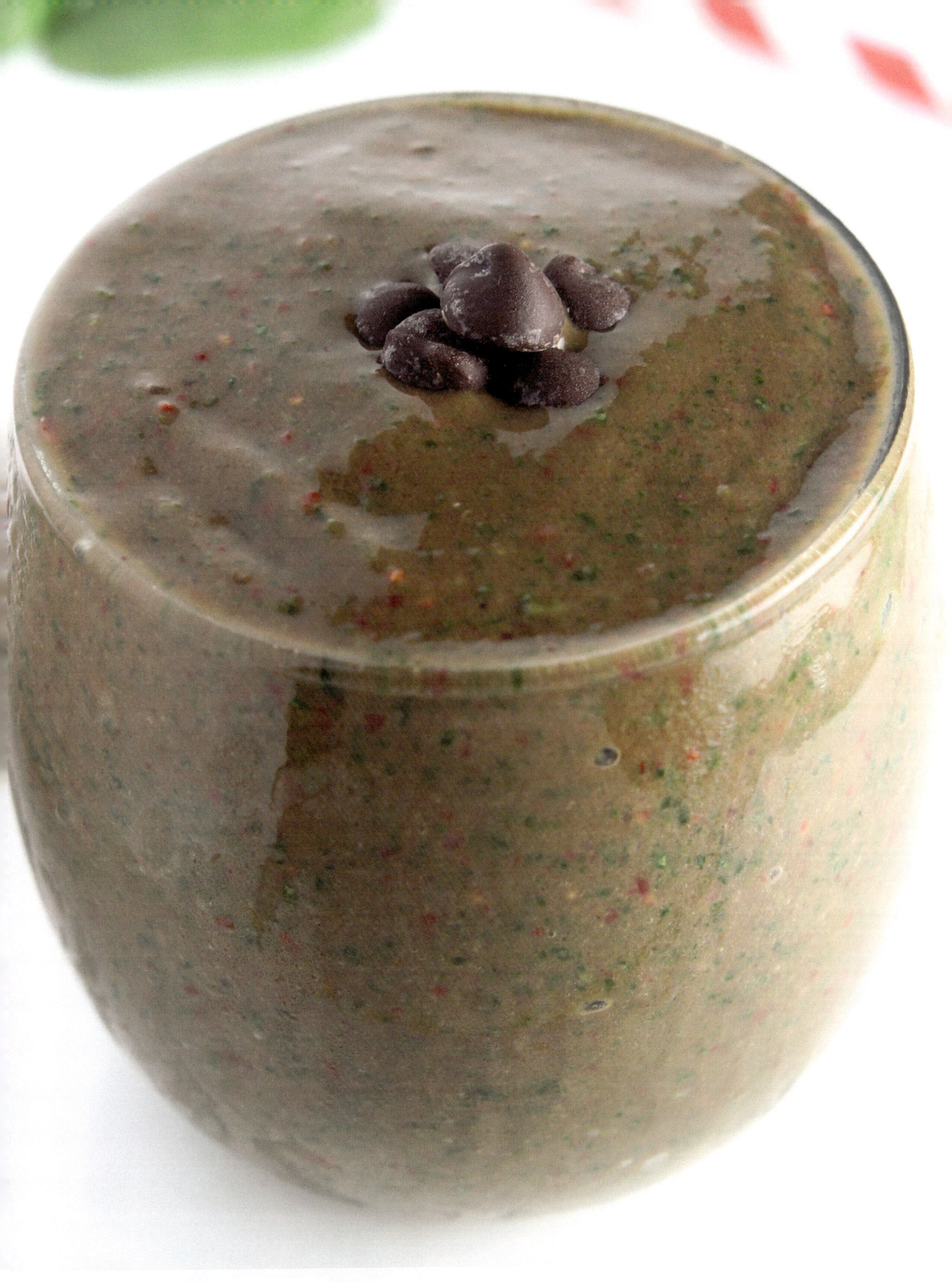

SKINNY DOUBLE CHOCOLATE FRAPPUCCINO

prep time: 5 minutes ♥ yields: 1 frappuccino

As a latecomer to the coffee game, I sampled my first frappuccino just two years ago from a shop located a few blocks down the street. Since temperatures consistently reach 100°F during our summers, that sweet blended drink was a very welcome treat! Because I knew my wallet would complain if I ordered one every day, I came up with my own recipes to make at home, and this has always been one of my favorites.

- ¾ cup (180mL) extra-strong coffee, chilled
- ½ cup (120mL) nonfat milk
- 2 tbsp (10g) unsweetened cocoa powder
- 2 ¼ cups (290g) ice cubes
- 2 tsp Truvia®, or to taste
- ½ tsp miniature chocolate chips, chopped

1. Add the coffee, milk, cocoa powder, ice, and Truvia® to a blender, and pulse until smooth. Pour into a glass, and top with the chopped chocolate.

C   GF

Nutrition Information: 78 calories | 1.8g fat (0.4g saturated fat, 0.1g unsaturated fat) | 2.5mg cholesterol 191.5mg sodium | 13.6g carbohydrates (4.0g fiber, 7.6g sugar) | 6.2g protein

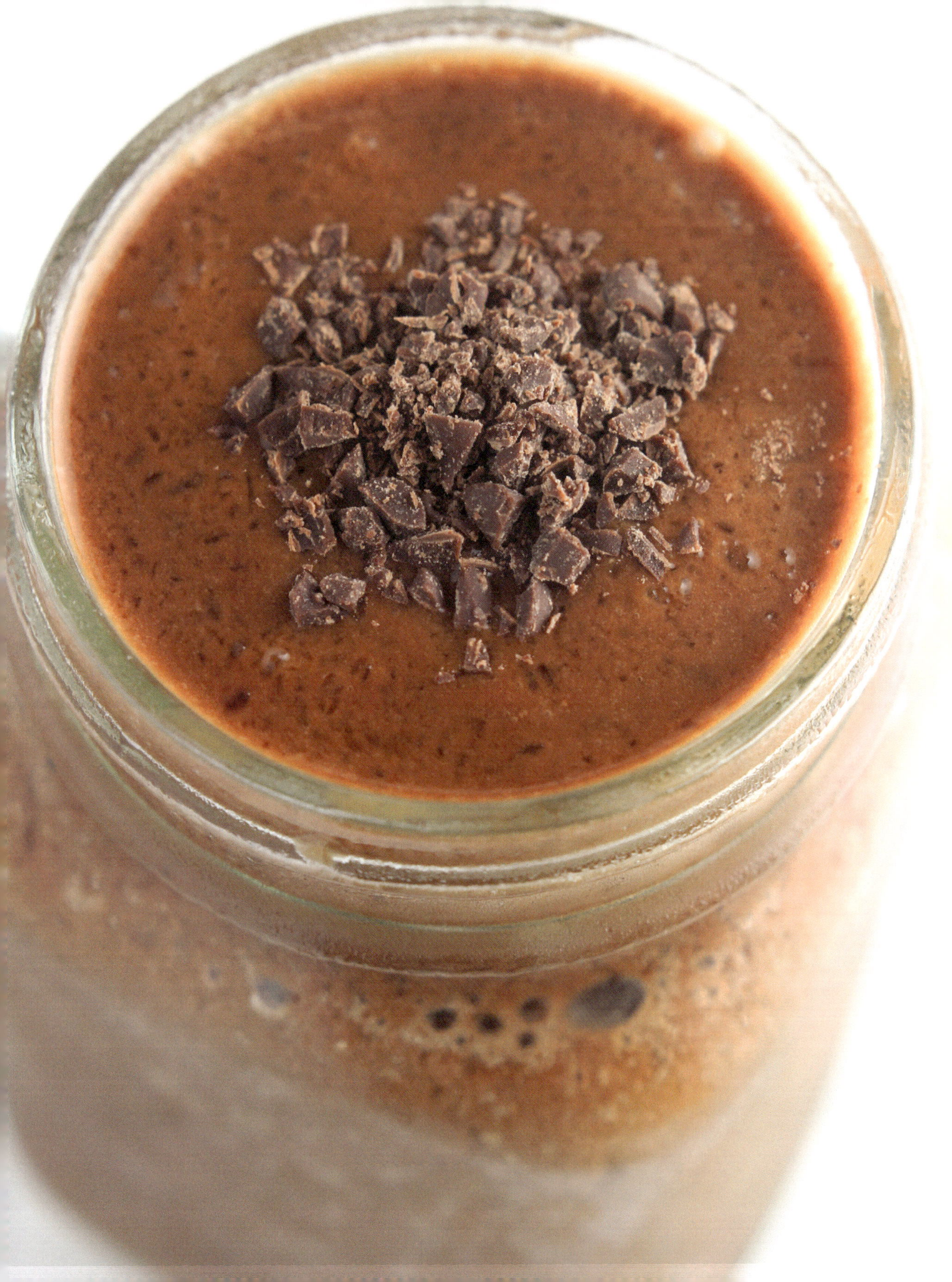

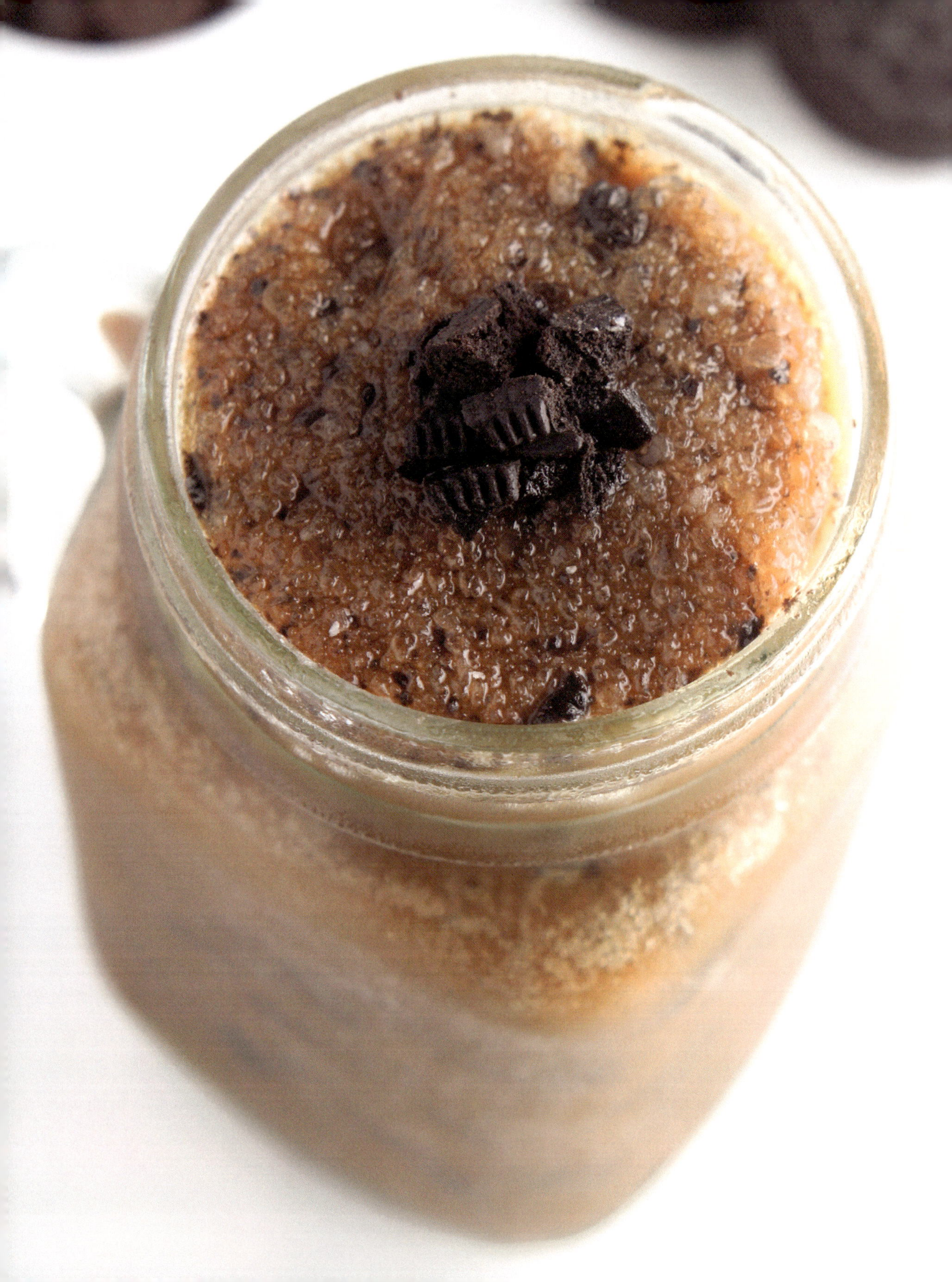

SKINNY COOKIES 'N CREAM FRAPPUCCINO

prep time: 5 minutes ♥ yields: 1 frappuccino

While growing up, I always looked forward to the nights where my mom would scoop a serving of cookies 'n cream ice cream for my brother and me after dinner. We usually slurped up the plain ice cream and set aside the biggest cookie chunks for last. But I always thought of ice cream as a nighttime dessert until one of my college friends mentioned that she would eat a bowl for breakfast after slumber parties in middle school! Since that felt like it broke all of the breakfast rules, this lighter frappuccino is my happy compromise.

- ¾ cup (180mL) extra-strong coffee, chilled
- ½ cup (120mL) nonfat milk
- 2 tbsp (10g) unsweetened cocoa powder
- 1 ½ tbsp (6g) sugar-free, fat-free instant vanilla pudding mix
- 1 tsp Truvia®, or to taste
- 1 ¾ cups (230g) ice cubes
- 2 chocolate sandwich cookies, cream filling removed and chopped

1. Add the coffee, milk, cocoa powder, instant pudding mix, Truvia®, and ice cubes to a blender. Pulse until smooth. Add the chopped chocolate cookies, and pulse twice. Pour the frappuccino into a glass.

Nutrition Information: 128 calories | 3.1g fat (0.1g saturated fat, 0.2g unsaturated fat) | 2.5mg cholesterol 457.2mg sodium | 33.2g carbohydrates (4.0g fiber, 6.2g sugar) | 6.2g protein

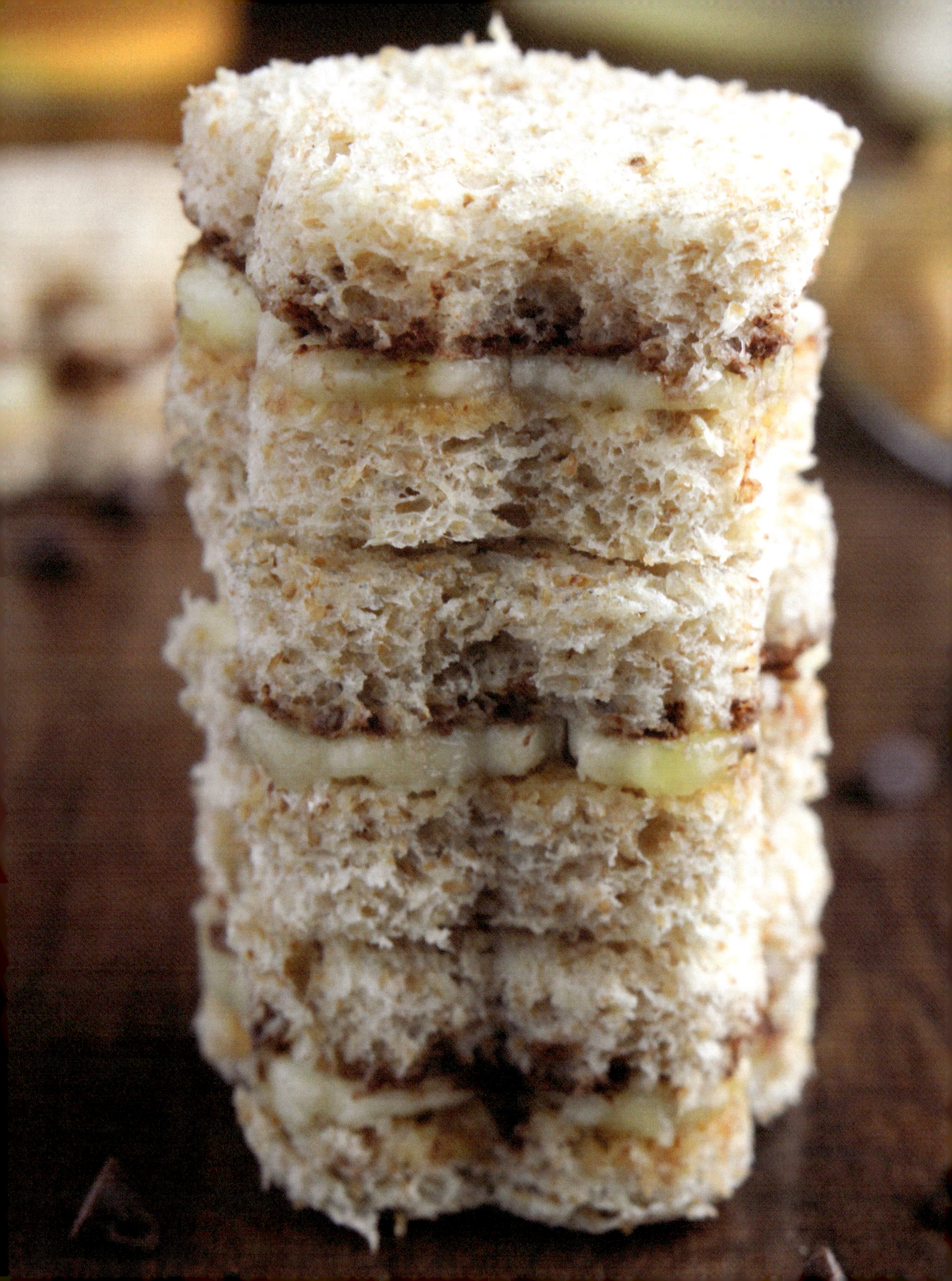

SNACKS

♥ ♥ ♥

Every afternoon when I arrived home from school, I walked into the pantry to rummage around for a snack. I normally gravitated towards the granola bars, especially the ones with big chocolate chunks, but pretzels and crackers usually won out for my brother. Occasionally, we somehow managed to sneak a chocolate chip cookie, too! The following recipes are some of my favorite snacks, although many are healthier versions of what I munched on during my childhood.

CHOCOLATE FLAX CRACKERS

prep time: 20 minutes ♥ baking time: 30-35 minutes ♥ yields: 8 servings

Throughout my childhood, my mom paid for a membership at one of the city pools, and we drove over nearly every afternoon to splash around and dive for toy rings we tossed across the bottom. During the 15-minute adult swim periods, Mom would jump in to do freestyle laps, and she always packed a snack to keep us kids entertained. We often found pouches of fruit snacks or cinnamon graham crackers in the tote bag, but the chocolate graham crackers were our favorite. These healthier crackers almost taste like a miniature version of them!

- 1 ¾ cups (210g) whole wheat flour
- ¼ cup (20g) unsweetened cocoa powder
- ¼ cup (26g) flaxseed meal
- ½ tsp salt
- 2 tsp coconut oil, melted
- ¼ cup (60mL) agave
- ½ cup (120mL) water, room temperature

1. Preheat the oven to 350°F, and set out two silicone baking mats and baking sheets. Alternatively, cut two sheets of parchment paper the same size as two baking sheets.
2. Whisk together the flour, cocoa powder, flaxseed meal, and salt in a medium bowl. Make a well in the center, and pour in the coconut oil, agave, and water. Stir until all of the dry ingredients have been completely incorporated.
3. Divide the dough in half. Working with one half at a time, place it onto one silicone baking mat, and roll to 1/16" thickness. Using a pizza wheel or a very sharp knife, slice the dough into 1"-thick vertical strips, followed by 1"-thick horizontal strips, to create the square crackers. Prick the center of each cracker with a fork.
4. Slide the silicone baking mats onto the baking sheets. Bake the crackers at 350°F for 30-35 minutes or until the crackers are crunchy. Cool the crackers completely to room temperature on the baking sheets.

C DF V

Nutrition Information: 149 calories | 3.0g fat (1.2g saturated fat, 0.1g unsaturated fat) | 0.0mg cholesterol 177.8mg sodium | 29.8g carbohydrates (5.2g fiber, 8.0g sugar) | 4.8g protein

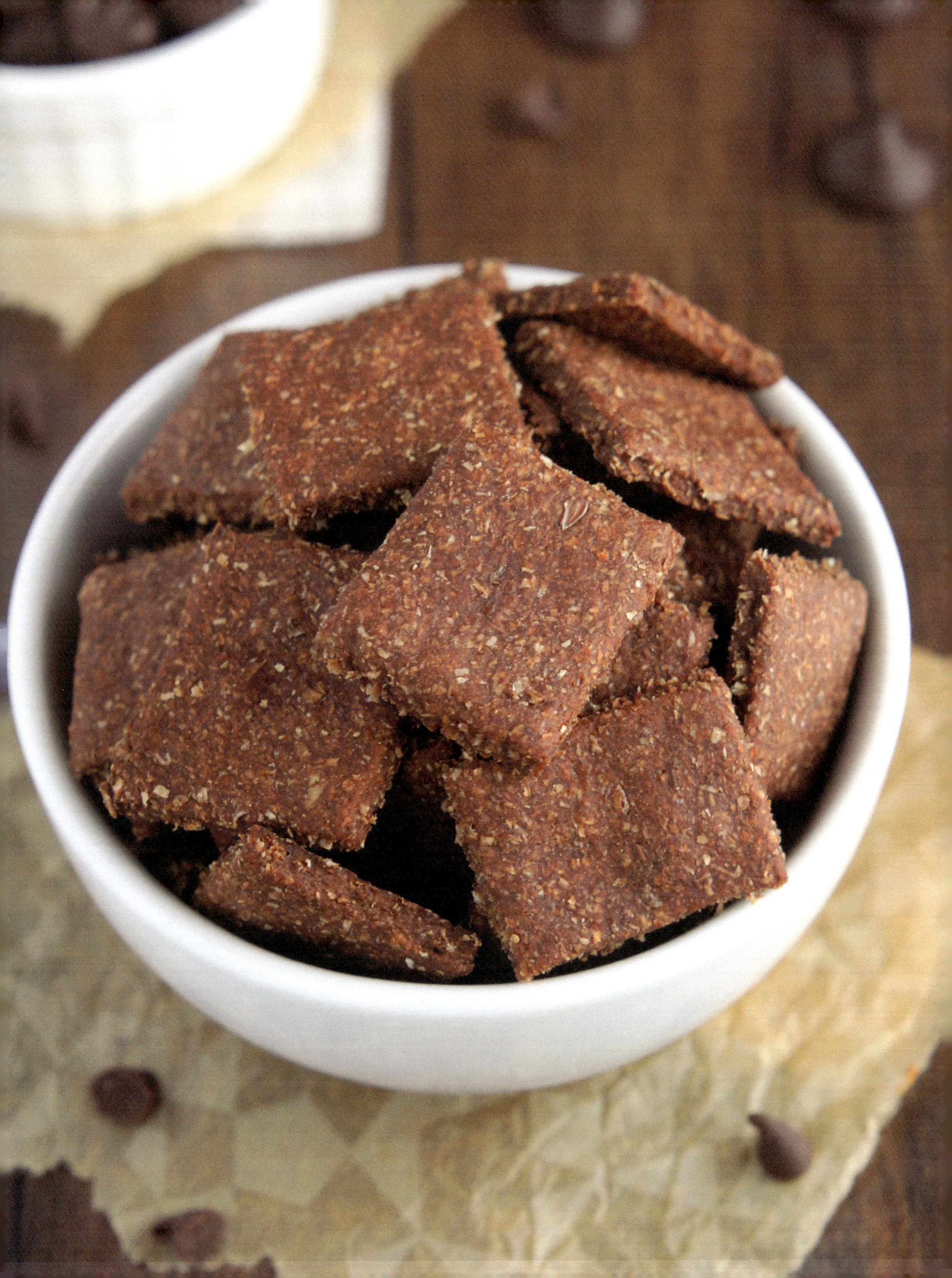

PUMPKIN CHOCOLATE CHIP GRANOLA BARS

prep time: 10 minutes ♥ baking time: 10-13 minutes ♥ yields: 10 bars

My dad packed a brown bag lunch for me nearly every day of high school. In addition to the healthy meal, he also tucked a granola bar inside for a mid-morning snack, generally a Quaker® Chewy one filled with chocolate, and I slowly nibbled on them, saving the bites with the biggest chocolate chunks for last. These are a much healthier version, made with cozy fall flavors instead.

1 tsp coconut oil, melted
½ cup (122g) pumpkin purée
6 tbsp (90mL) nonfat milk
2 tbsp (30mL) maple syrup
1 ½ tsp ground cinnamon
2 ½ cups (250g) old-fashioned oats
¼ cup (56g) miniature chocolate chips

1. Preheat the oven to 300°F, and lightly coat an 8"-square pan with nonstick cooking spray.
2. Stir together the coconut oil and pumpkin purée in a medium bowl. Add the milk, maple syrup and cinnamon, stirring until thoroughly combined. Add the oats, mixing until completely incorporated. Fold in the miniature chocolate chips.
3. Gently press the mixture into the prepared pan. Bake at 300°F for 10-13 minutes or until just firm to the touch. Cool completely in the pan before slicing into 10 bars.

AMY'S ADVICE
For an easy on-the-go snack, wrap each individual granola bar in plastic wrap before storing in the refrigerator.

C

Nutrition Information: 125 calories | 3.6g fat (1.2g saturated fat, 1.0g unsaturated fat) | 0.2mg cholesterol
4.8mg sodium | 21.4g carbohydrates (2.7g fiber, 7.0g sugar) | 3.0g protein

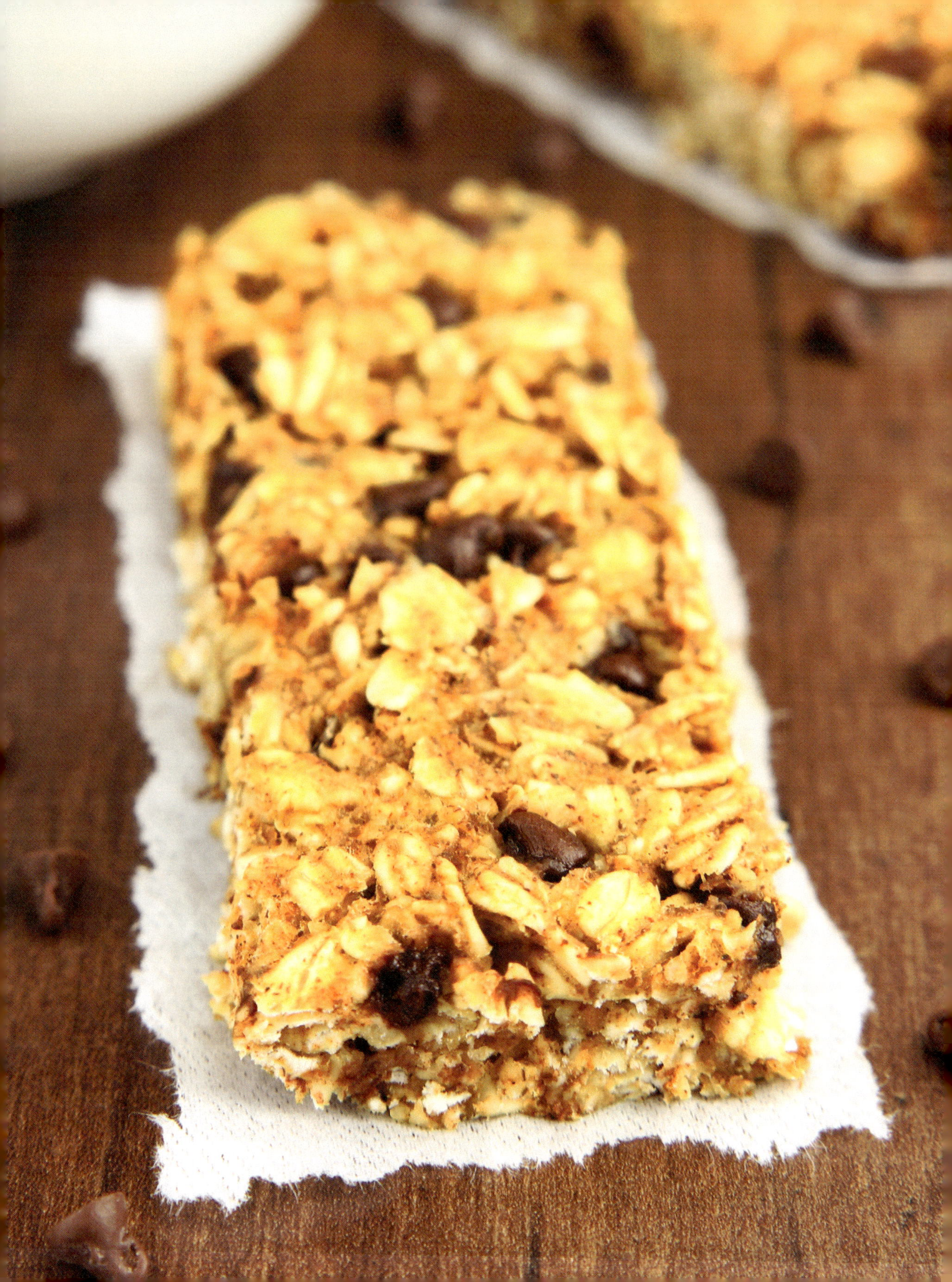

DARK CHOCOLATE BLUEBERRY GRANOLA BARS

prep time: 10 minutes ♥ baking time: 11-14 minutes ♥ yields: 10 bars

A few times each semester, I played the flute in our high school musicals and band concerts. The directors required that we arrived a few hours early to each performance, starting around 5 pm, which left no time in the evening for a real dinner. Instead, I usually tucked a Clif® Bar into my purse to nibble on backstage. With plenty of shows each year, I tried a variety of flavors, but the chocolate chip, blueberry crisp, and chocolate brownie were my favorites. They served as the inspiration for this recipe—just without the flute and solos!

1 tsp coconut oil, melted
½ cup (120g) unsweetened applesauce, room temperature
3 tbsp (15g) unsweetened cocoa powder
½ cup (120mL) nonfat milk, room temperature
1 tbsp (15mL) agave
2 ½ cups (250g) old-fashioned oats
¼ cup (40g) dried wild blueberries

1. Preheat the oven to 300°F, and lightly coat an 8"-square pan with nonstick cooking spray.
2. Stir together the coconut oil, applesauce, and cocoa powder in a medium bowl. Add the milk and agave, stirring until thoroughly combined. Add the oats, mixing until completely incorporated. Fold in the dried blueberries.
3. Gently press the mixture into the prepared pan. Bake at 300°F for 11-14 minutes or until just firm to the touch. Cool completely in the pan before slicing into 10 bars.

AMY'S ADVICE
For an easy on-the-go snack, wrap each individual granola bar in plastic wrap before storing in the refrigerator.

C

Nutrition Information: 115 calories | 2.2g fat (0.4g saturated fat, 1.0g unsaturated fat) | 0.3mg cholesterol 25.1mg sodium | 23.5g carbohydrates (3.3g fiber, 7.5g sugar) | 3.3g protein

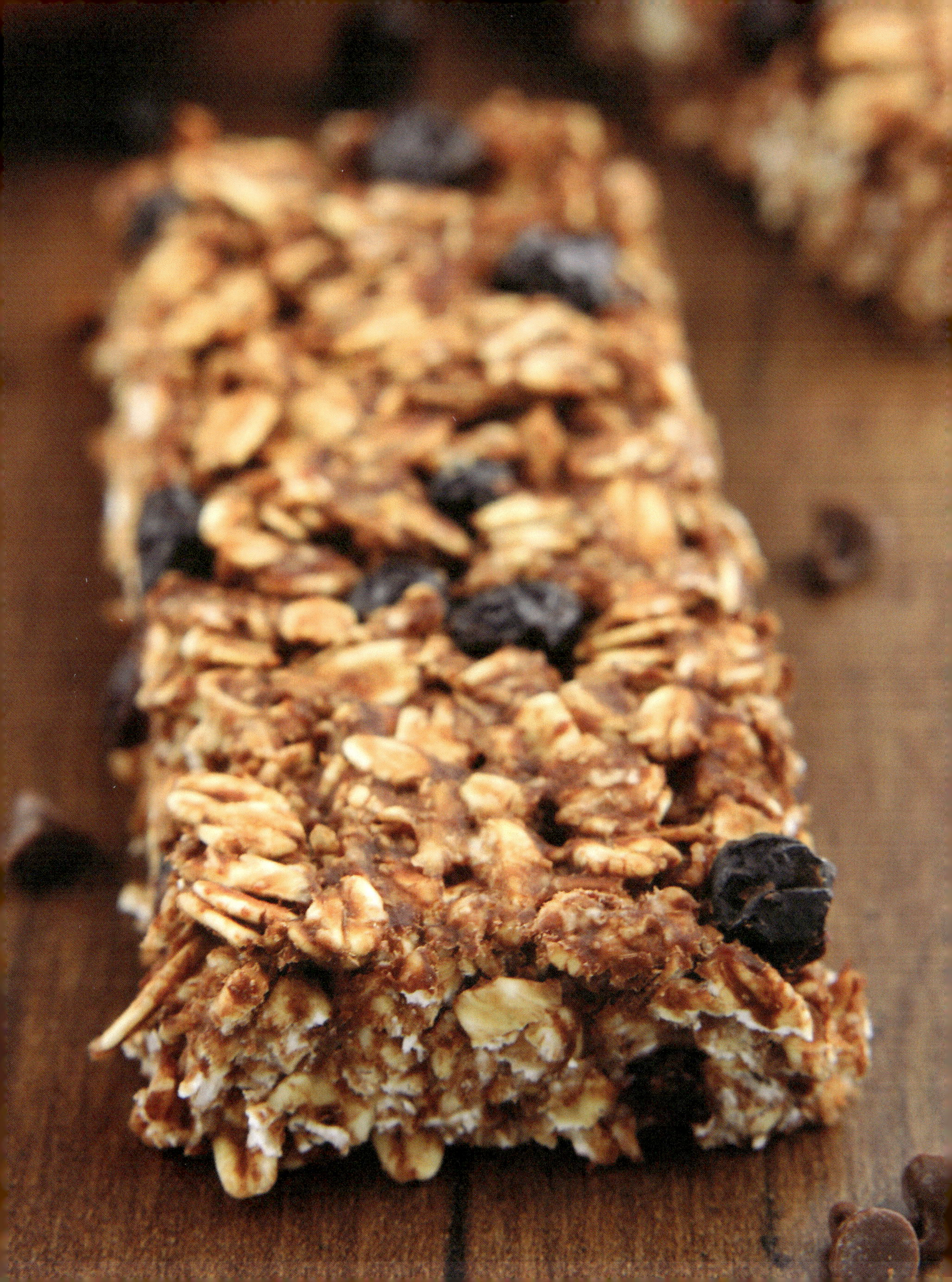

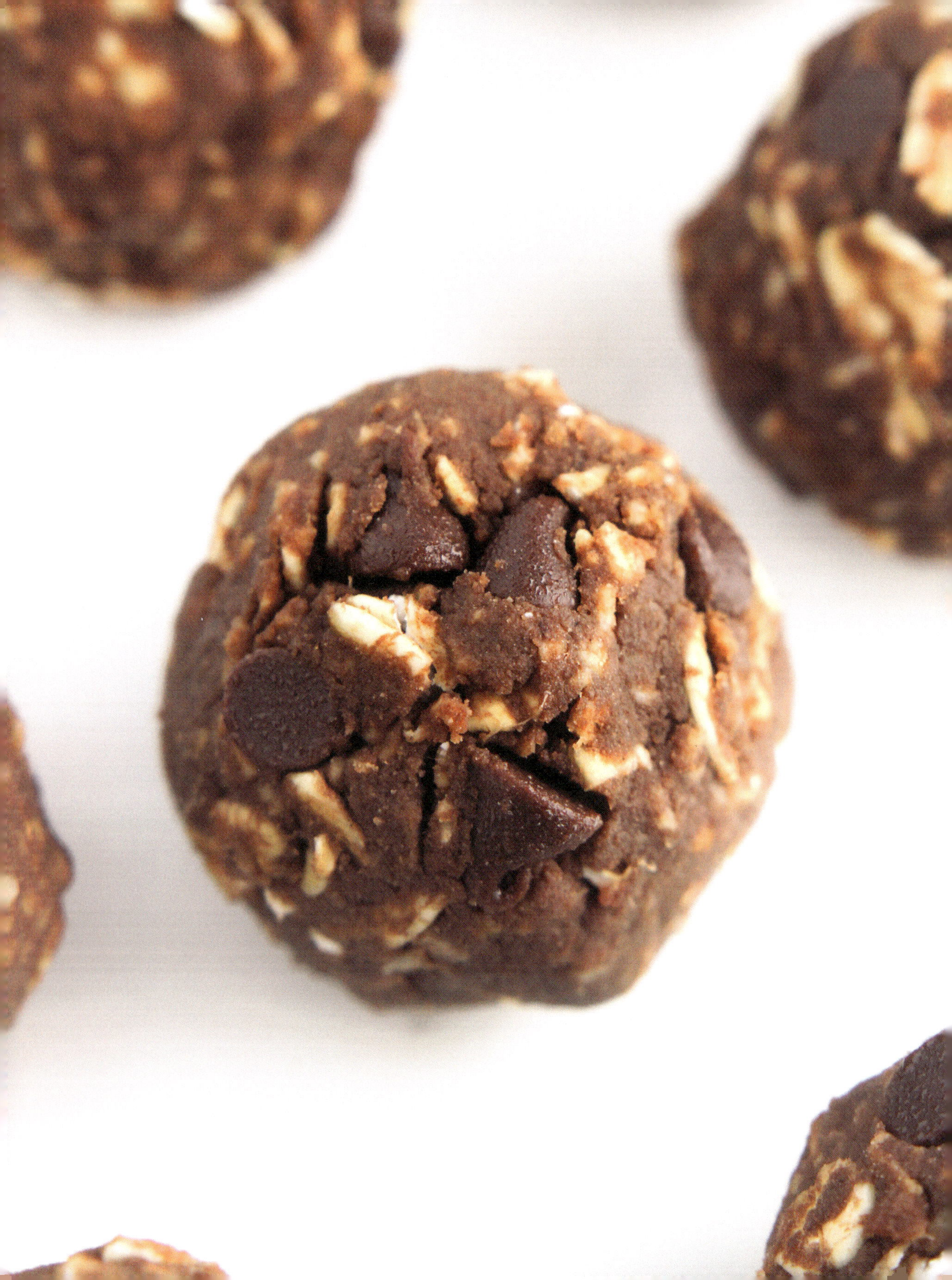

CHOCOLATE DATE ENERGY BITES

prep time: 25 minutes ♥ inactive time: 20 minutes ♥ yields: 8 servings

One of my dad's college friends is an ultrarunner and regularly participates in 100-mile races around the country, including steep trails in the Utah mountains. On one of his trips to visit my family, he didn't skip a beat of training and ran 25-30 miles each day, fueled by his favorite "goo"—a blend of honey, fruit juices, and electrolytes. Although "goo" powered him through his workouts, I prefer chewing on a healthy snack for mine, like these chocolaty protein-packed energy

- ½ cup (80g) dried pitted dates
- 1 cup (240mL) water
- 1 cup (100g) old-fashioned oats
- 2 scoops (60g) PlantFusion® Vanilla Bean protein powder
- ¼ cup (20g) unsweetened cocoa powder
- 2 tbsp (28g) miniature chocolate chips

1. Add the dates and water to a large microwave-safe bowl, and cover the top with a tight-fitting lid or plastic wrap. Microwave the bowl on HIGH for 1 minute. Let the mixture cool for 5 minutes before adding the hydrated dates and ¼ cup of the remaining liquid to a food processor. Pulse until smooth. Let the mixture cool completely to room temperature. Optional: Place in the refrigerator to speed up the process.
2. Add the oats, protein powder, and cocoa powder to a medium bowl, and stir until thoroughly combined. Mix in the date paste and another 6 tablespoons of the liquid, stirring until fully incorporated. Stir in the miniature chocolate chips.
3. Shape the chocolate mixture into 32 balls, and place each in a large airtight container after rolling. Cover with the lid, and store the energy bites in the refrigerator until ready to serve.

AMY'S ADVICE
This recipe only works with plant-based protein powders!

C   DF   V   HP

Nutrition Information: 118 calories | 2.6g fat (0.5g saturated fat, 0.4g unsaturated fat) | 0.0mg cholesterol
130.2mg sodium | 19.0g carbohydrates (2.8g fiber, 9.6g sugar) | 7.3g protein

CHOCOLATE CHIP SOFT PRETZEL BITES

prep time: 40 minutes ♥ baking time: 6-8 minutes ♥ yields: 16 servings

My dad and I are huge baseball fans, and we're in the process of visitng all 30 Major League Baseball stadiums around America together. As of this cookbook's publishing date, we've already attended games at 22! Although Dad looks forward to hot dogs and sausages, I prefer less greasy stadium food, so I often turn to soft pretzels. While watching the ballgame and scribbling the plays in my scorecard, I tear the pretzel into small, bite-sized pieces, and one time, I imagined how much easier it would be if the vendors sold pretzel bites instead. These are my healthier version of what I envisioned, complete with chocolate chips!

for the pretzels
- 1 cup (240mL) warm water (100-110°F)
- 2 tsp coconut oil, melted
- 2 tsp agave
- ½ tsp salt
- 2 ¼ tsp (one ¼ oz package) active dry yeast
- 3 ½ - 4 cups (420-480g) whole wheat flour
- ¼ cup (56g) miniature chocolate chips

for the wash
- 3 cups (720mL) hot water
- ¼ cup (19g) baking soda
- 2-3 tbsp (34-50g) coarse sea salt

C DF V

Nutrition Information: 120 calories | 2.1g fat (1.1g saturated fat, 0.1g unsaturated fat) 0.0mg cholesterol | 72.7mg sodium 23.5g carbohydrates (3.4g fiber, 2.7g sugar) 3.8g protein

1. Stir together the water, oil, agave, and salt in a medium bowl. Stir in the yeast, and let the mixture sit for 10-15 minutes or until frothy. Mix in 3 cups of flour, 1 cup at a time, until a wet dough forms. Mix in the miniature chocolate chips.

2. Turn the dough out onto a well-floured surface, and knead for 3-5 minutes or until the dough springs back most of the way when you gently press your index finger into it. Let the dough rest while completing the next step.

3. Preheat the oven to 425°F. Line two baking sheets with foil, and generously coat with nonstick cooking spray.

4. Divide the dough in half. Working with one half at a time, evenly divide the dough into 8 pieces. Roll each piece into a 4"-long log, and slice each log into 4 pieces with a sharp knife. Place the bites onto a separate well-floured surface while slicing the rest of the dough.

5. To prepare the wash, add the baking soda to a medium bowl, and carefully pour in the hot water. Stir to fully dissolve the baking soda.

6. Working with 2-3 pretzel bites at a time, place them onto a slotted spatula or spoon, and briefly dip them into the wash. Place them on the prepared baking sheets, and sprinkle with coarse sea salt.

7. Bake the pretzel bites at 425°F for 6-8 minutes or until light golden brown. Cool the bites on the pan for at least 5 minutes.

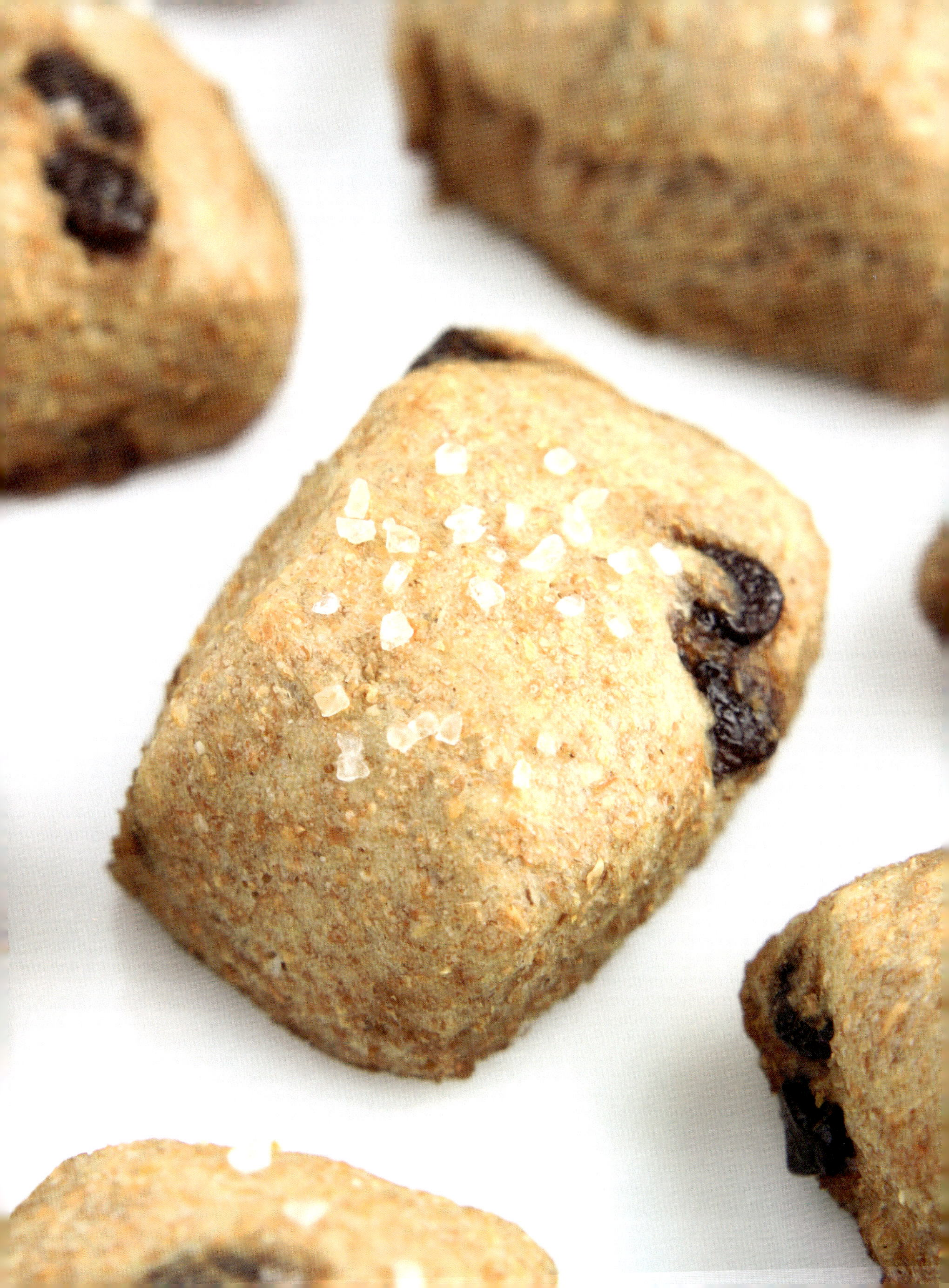

CHOCOLATE KETTLE CORN

prep time: 2 minutes ♥ cooking time: 10-15 minutes ♥ yields: 4 servings

At the Farmer's Market in my hometown, stands selling fresh fruit, vegetables, and flower bouquets fill the sidewalks of one narrow downtown street. At the end of the row sits a booth that sells freshly popped kettle corn, and its sweet aroma always fills the air, easily attracting the most customers and resulting in the longest line on the block. As much as I adore kettle corn, I rarely had the patience to wait in that line, so I started making my own at home. I've created a few different flavor twists, but this chocolate version is one of my favorites!

½ cup (70g) popcorn kernels
3 tbsp (36g) granulated sugar
¼ tsp salt
½ tsp coconut oil
2 tsp unsweetened cocoa powder

1. Set aside 3 popcorn kernels. Combine the remaining popcorn kernels, sugar, and salt in a small bowl.
2. Add the coconut oil to a medium pot, and melt over medium-low heat. Once melted, add 3 popcorn kernels and cover with the lid. While holding the lid, shake the pot back and forth every 2-3 seconds until the kernels have popped. Take the pot off of the heat, and carefully remove the popped kernels.
3. Add the remaining popcorn kernels, and stir with a spatula until they're evenly coated with the sugar and salt. Return the pot to the heat, cover, and continue shaking it every 2-3 seconds until at least 3 seconds elapse in between pops. Immediate pour the popcorn into a large bowl, sprinkle the cocoa powder on top, and toss until it's evenly coated.

AMY'S ADVICE
Add a few shakes of cinnamon for a warm spice flavor!

GF DF V

Nutrition Information: 107 calories | 1.5g fat (0.6g saturated fat, 0.5g unsaturated fat) | 0.0mg cholesterol 178.5mg sodium | 23.4g carbohydrates (3.4g fiber, 9.5g sugar) | 2.4g protein

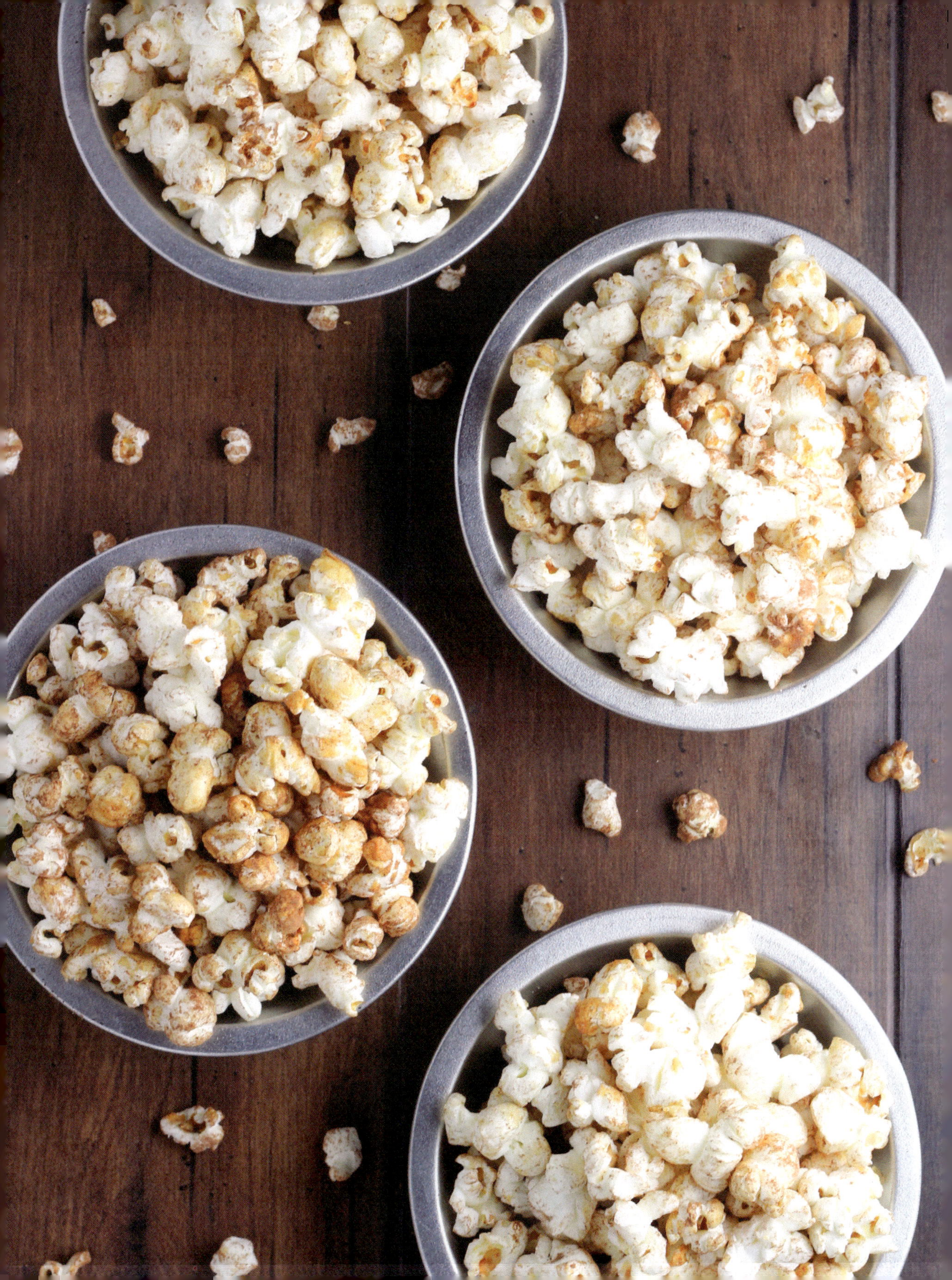

DARK CHOCOLATE CINNAMON MUDDY BUDDIES

prep time: 15 minutes ♥ baking time: 40-45 minutes ♥ yields: 10 servings

After carpooling home from elementary school with a friend one day, her mom set out a large zip-topped plastic bag on the kitchen table with an afternoon snack enclosed for us. Confused, I peeked inside and saw cereal squares covered in powdered sugar. I cautiously took a bite... And then grabbed a big fistful when I tasted the chocolate and peanut butter coating. That was one of my few encounters with muddy buddies (also called puppy chow), but it was too irresistible and addictive to make at home! Many years later as a food blogger, I finally created a lighter version with the same sweet crunch and just a fraction of

6 cups (186g) rice pocket cereal (such as Rice Chex™)
2 tbsp (16g) cornstarch
1 cup (240mL) nonfat milk
½ cup (112g) dark chocolate chips, melted
½ cup (60g) powdered sugar
1 tsp ground cinnamon

1. Preheat the oven to 350°F, and lightly coat a 9"x13" baking pan with nonstick cooking spray. Add the cereal to a large bowl.
2. In a small bowl, whisk together the cornstarch and 2 tablespoons of milk until a slurry forms. Add the remaining milk to a small pot, and cook over medium-low heat, stirring frequently, until it begins to simmer. Reduce the heat to low. While stirring constantly, slowly pour in the cornstarch slurry in a thin stream. Continue to stir for 1 more minute or until the mixture begins to thicken.
3. Remove the pot from the heat, and add the melted dark chocolate. Stir until the chocolate is mostly incorporated. Return the pot to the burner over low heat, and continue stirring for another 2 minutes or until it reaches the consistency of thin pudding.
4. Pour the chocolate mixture over the cereal, and gently toss with a spatula until the cereal is coated. Transfer the cereal to the prepared pan, and bake at 350°F for a total of 45-50 minutes, stirring after the first 15 minutes. After 30 minutes of baking have elapsed, let the cereal cool for 3 minutes before breaking apart any clumps. Continue baking for another 15-20 minutes, or until the cereal is crunchy.

AMY'S ADVICE
It's REALLY important to constantly stir while adding the cornstarch slurry! If you stop stirring at any point, you'll end up with big clumps in your milk and will need to start over.

GF

Nutrition Information: 150 calories | 3.6g fat (2.4g saturated fat, 0.0g unsaturated fat) | 0.5mg cholesterol 158.4mg sodium | 28.6g carbohydrates (1.5g fiber, 12.8g sugar) | 2.0g protein

5. While the cereal mixture bakes, add the powdered sugar and cinnamon to a large zip-topped bag. After the cereal has finished baking and has cooled for 5 minutes, pour it into the bag with the powdered sugar. Seal the top, and shake until all of the cereal is coated. Discard any remaining powdered sugar, and leave the top of the bag open while the cereal cools.

CIRCUS ANIMAL SNACK MIX

prep time: 4 minutes ♥ yields: 6 servings

This past New Year's Eve, my mom bought tickets for our family to see Cirque du Soleil. Despite our love for shows and musicals, none of us had seen Cirque du Soleil in person. Throughout the entire performance, we all sat on the edges of our seats, often with our mouths halfway open, completely amazed by the impressive—and somewhat dangerous—gymnastic feats by the performers. During one set change, a man came onto the stage and conducted an invisible circus, complete with growling bears, chattering monkeys, and slowly plodding elephants. That Cirque du Soleil act and the invisible animals served as the inspiration for this fun snack mix!

1 ¾ cups (90g) animal crackers
¾ cup (60g) chocolate bear graham crackers (such as Teddy Grahams®)
¼ cup (28g) low-fat banana chips, chopped
3 tbsp (28g) lightly salted peanuts

1. Add all of the ingredients to a large zip-topped bag. Seal and gently toss.

AMY'S ADVICE
Try substituting cashews or slivered almonds for the peanuts!

DF

Nutrition Information: 153 calories | 5.5g fat (0.8g saturated fat, 1.2g unsaturated fat) | 0.0mg cholesterol | 120.0mg sodium | 23.8g carbohydrates (1.8g fiber, 8.5g sugar) | 2.8g protein

CHOCOLATE PRETZEL GORP

prep time: 4 minutes ♥ yields: 6 servings

Throughout my childhood, my family went camping in the Sierra Nevada Mountains at least twice each summer. We pitched a tent, set sleeping bags on top of thin mattress pads, and spent the days hiking dusty trails and swimming in icy cold lakes. All of that exercise really worked up our appetites, so my mom always brought along bags of GORP: Good Ol' Raisins and Peanuts. While she left the adult batch as classic as its name, she usually added a few extra treats to the kid bag, and this version of her GORP was my favorite.

2 cups (90g) miniature pretzel twists
¼ cup (36g) raisins
3 tbsp (28g) lightly salted peanuts
2 tbsp (28g) miniature chocolate chips

1. Add all of the ingredients to a large zip-topped bag. Seal and gently toss.

AMY'S ADVICE
We also love substituting dried cranberries for the raisins!

DF V

Nutrition Information: 125 calories | 3.7g fat (1.0g saturated fat, 1.2g unsaturated fat) | 0.0mg cholesterol 139.1mg sodium | 21.1g carbohydrates (1.1g fiber, 6.9g sugar) | 2.9g protein

SNACKS ♥ 63

STRAWBERRY DIP WITH CHOCOLATE BEAR DUNKERS

prep time: 5 minutes ♥ yields: 4 servings

In college, quite a few of the food options offered in the dining hall for dinner looked too greasy or unhealthy for my tastes, so I often made my own meal at the salad bar instead. I loaded up a big plate (or two) with spinach, vegetables, and a sprinkling of cheese and nuts. Since the kitchen left the tubs of dressings unlabeled, I usually skipped them, but one night I felt adventurous and dabbed a little of each onto a plate for dipping carrot sticks. When I reached the slightly pink one, my mouth did a double-take—it was strawberry yogurt! While carrot and strawberry yogurt dip may have been a bad idea, chocolate crackers make for a much tastier combination.

⅔ cup (95g) fresh strawberries, sliced
1 cup (240g) plain nonfat Greek yogurt
1 tbsp (13g) Truvia®
½ cup (60g) chocolate bear graham crackers (such as Teddy Grahams®)

1. Add the strawberries to a food processor or blender, and pulse until puréed. Add the purée to a medium bowl, and stir in the Greek yogurt and Truvia®. Serve with the chocolate bear graham crackers.

AMY'S ADVICE
Sometimes I skip the chocolate bear dunkers and eat this dip for breakfast!

HP

Nutrition Information: 107 calories | 2.3g fat (0.5g saturated fat, 0.0g unsaturated fat) | 0.0mg cholesterol 106.5mg sodium | 14.9g carbohydrates (1.5g fiber, 7.5g sugar) | 6.9g protein

STRAWBERRY HAZELNUT QUESADILLAS

prep time: 5 minutes ♥ yields: 4 servings

For my mom's birthday last year, a friend gave her a gigantic 10-pound jar of Nutella®. It was bigger than my head! She patiently left it sitting on the pantry shelf untouched for nearly an entire month, waiting until my brother and I returned home for the holidays so our entire family could enjoy it together. We ceremoniously opened it to drizzle over fresh crêpes with sliced strawberries made by my brother on New Year's Day. Our love for strawberries and Nutella® must be hereditary! Since I sometimes lack the patience to cook crêpes from scratch like my brother, I substitute a folded tortilla for this quick and easy snack.

2 whole wheat tortillas, soft taco size
4 tsp chocolate hazelnut spread (such as Nutella®)
½ cup (100g) thinly sliced fresh strawberries

1. Working with one tortilla at a time, spread 2 teaspoons of chocolate hazelnut spread across the bottom half of the tortilla. Arrange half of the sliced strawberries on top. Fold over the top half of the tortilla, and gently press down. Repeat with the remaining ingredients.

AMY'S ADVICE
We love making these quesadillas with just about every kind of fresh fruit!

Nutrition Information: 106 calories | 3.4g fat (1.1g saturated fat, 0.5g unsaturated fat) | 0.0mg cholesterol 197.7mg sodium | 16.4g carbohydrates (2.2g fiber, 5.3g sugar) | 2.1g protein

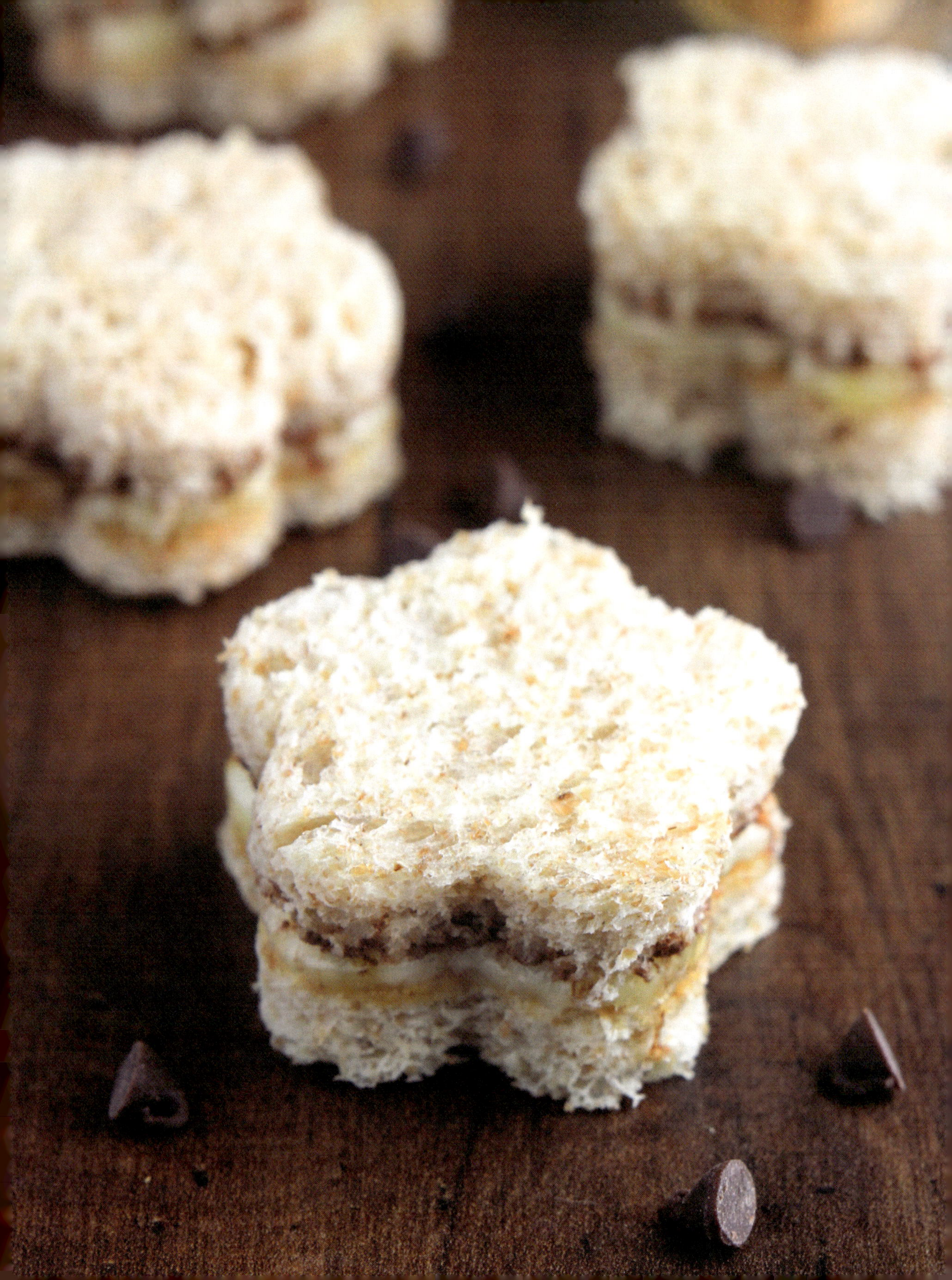

CHOCOLATE ELVIS SANDWICHES

prep time: 10 minutes ♥ yields: 4 servings

While I was growing up, everyone in my family preferred a different kind of peanut butter sandwich. I loved mine plain with creamy peanut butter; my dad ate the same, albeit with crunchy; my brother always requested his with honey; and my mom often added sliced bananas to hers. I eventually decided to try a bite of Mom's, and I quickly agreed that her combination was my second favorite. But when I recently added a dark chocolate drizzle, that immediately pushed it past my classic plain peanut butter sandwich into the #1 spot!

- 2 tbsp (10g) unsweetened cocoa powder
- 1 tsp honey
- 4 tsp nonfat milk
- 4 slices low-calorie double fiber whole wheat bread
- 1 tbsp (16g) natural creamy peanut butter
- 1 medium banana, thinly sliced

1. To prepare the chocolate drizzle, stir together the cocoa powder, honey, and milk in a small bowl until smooth.
2. Spread ½ tablespoon of peanut butter across 1 slice of bread. Layer half of the banana slices on top. Drizzle with half of the chocolate sauce, and top with another slice of bread. Repeat with the remaining ingredients. Cut the sandwiches into quarters or fun shapes with a cookie cutter.

AMY'S ADVICE
Try natural almond butter instead for a fun twist!

Nutrition Information: 112 calories | 2.9g fat (0.3g saturated fat, 0.0g unsaturated fat) 0.1mg cholesterol | 178.2mg sodium 23.8g carbohydrates (7.1g fiber, 6.3g sugar) 5.0g protein

COCOA SUGAR TORTILLA CHIPS

prep time: 5 minutes ♥ baking time: 18-20 minutes ♥ yields: 4 servings

As kids, my brother and I loved when my parents treated us to dinner at Chevys Fresh Mex®, a restaurant chain that served Mexican food with a California twist. At the Chevy's in our hometown, the owners set up a tortilla station in the back of the dining room. Whenever the kitchen ran out of fresh tortillas or chips, an employee would carry out a tray of dough balls, deftly slip them one by one into the flattening machine, and let them spin down the spiral conveyer belt inside while the hot coils cooked the tortillas. After ordering, my brother and I would stand in front of the machine, completely entranced, and often the employee would hand us each a ball of dough to play with. We never realized that we were depleting the stash of chips in the kitchen! Since we didn't like salsa, we rarely ate those tortilla chips, but if they had been covered in cocoa powder like these, that would've been an entirely different story.

4 whole wheat tortillas, soft taco size
2 tsp Truvia®
½ tsp cocoa powder

1. Preheat the oven to 350°F, and cover a large baking sheet foil. Lightly coat with nonstick cooking spray.
2. Slice the tortillas into 4 vertical strips, and slice each strip into triangles. Place the triangles onto the prepared baking sheet, and lightly coat them with nonstick cooking spray. Combine the Truvia® and cocoa powder in a small bowl, and sprinkle the mixture over the tortilla triangles.
3. Bake the tortilla triangles at 350°F for 18-20 minutes or until golden and beginning to lift up in the center. Cool on the baking sheet for 5 minutes before serving.

C   DF   V

Nutrition Information: 134 calories | 3.5g fat (1.0g saturated fat, 1.0g unsaturated fat) | 0.0mg cholesterol 392.7mg sodium | 22.1g carbohydrates (3.1g fiber, 1.0g sugar) | 3.0g protein

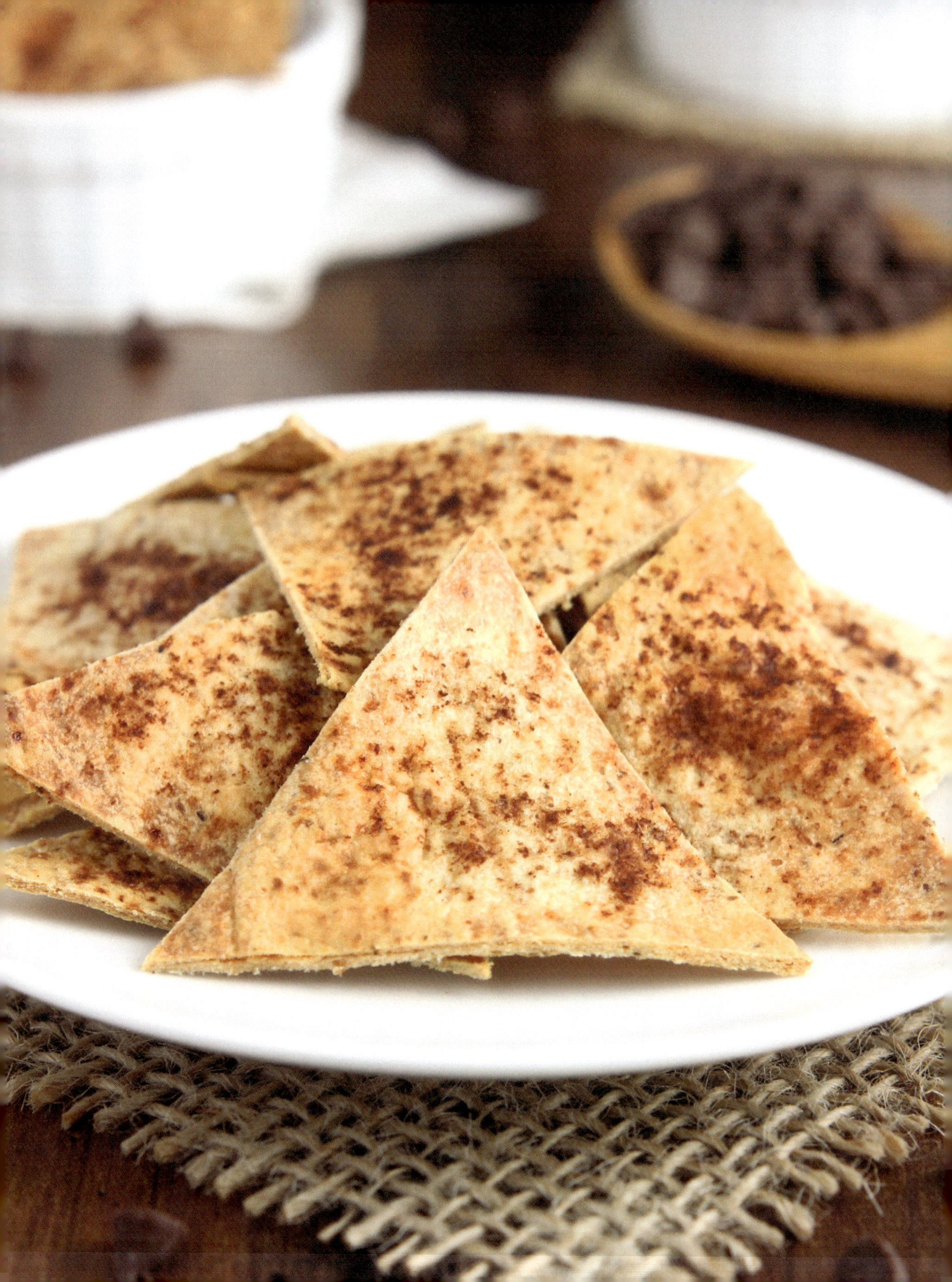

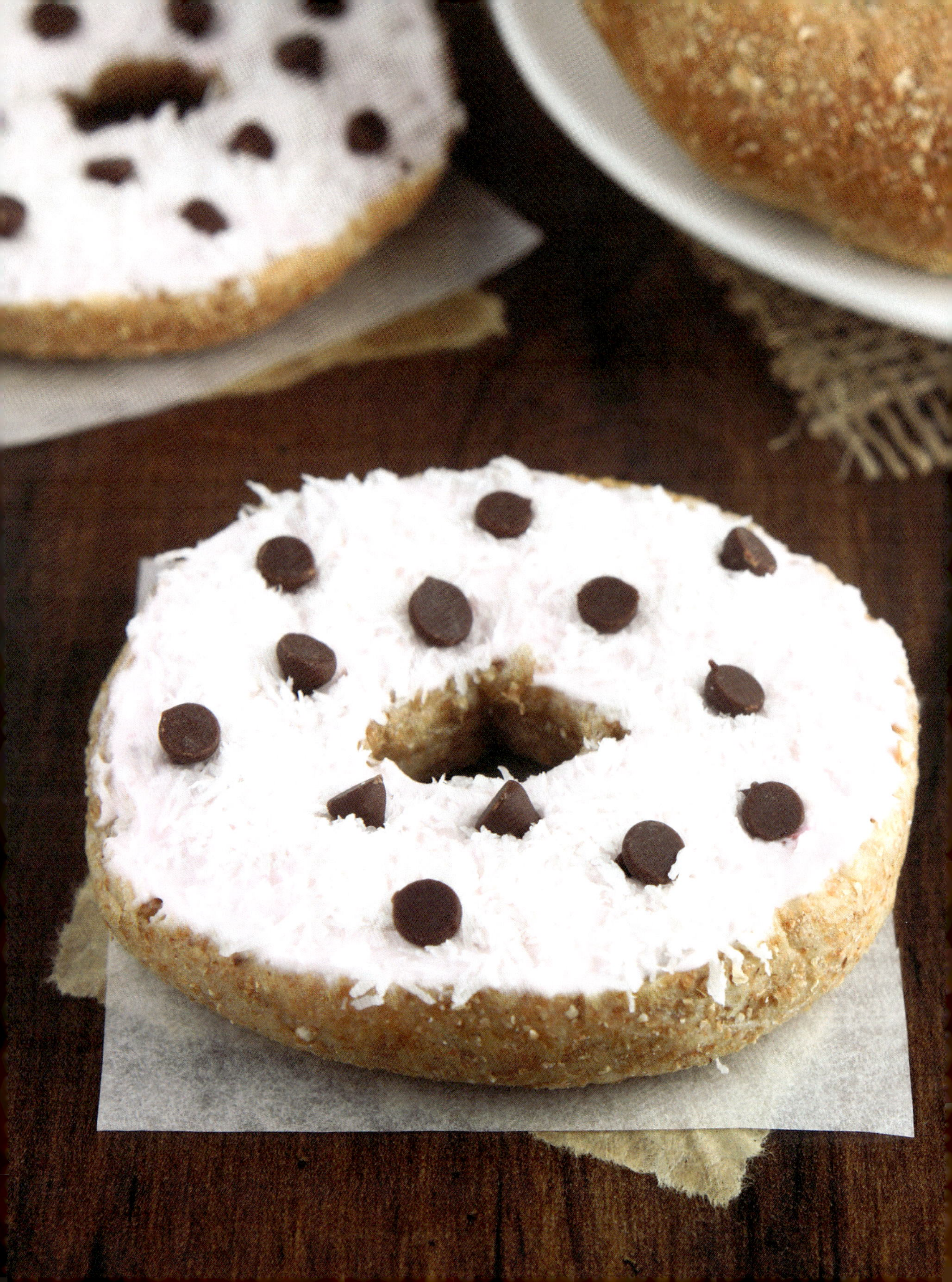

MINI STRAWBERRY "PIZZA" BAGELS

prep time: 10 minutes ♥ yields: 8 bagel halves

In graduate school, our Graduate Student Association set aside some of our student fees to fund "Free Bagel Fridays" each week. On those mornings, a few volunteers set up an oversized table in the student lounge loaded with platters of freshly baked bagels brought in from the gourmet shop downtown, along with a few toasters and multiple tubs of jam, peanut butter, and cream cheese. I rarely had the patience to wait in the toaster and schmear lines, so I usually nibbled on mine plain while sitting on the comfy couches and watching my friends wait their turns. One morning, I glanced down at a girl's toasted bagel covered in cream cheese and strawberry jam and thought, "That almost looks like a breakfast version of pizza bagel bites!" However, her bagel was missing the "pizza" toppings, so I added a few for these smaller, healthier ones.

4 miniature whole wheat bagels
½ cup (112g) Strawberry Dip (P.64)
8 tsp shredded unsweetened coconut
4 tsp miniature chocolate chips

1. Slice each bagel in half horizontally. Working with one bagel half at a time, spread 1 tablespoon of Strawberry Yogurt Dip across the cut side of the bagel. Sprinkle with 1 teaspoon of shredded coconut. Gently press ½ teaspoon of miniature chocolate chips on top. Repeat with the remaining ingredients.

AMY'S ADVICE
Try adding diced strawberries or apples as another "pizza" topping!

Nutrition Information: 87 calories | 2.4g fat (1.3g saturated fat, 0.0g unsaturated fat) | 0.0mg cholesterol
85.0mg sodium | 13.6g carbohydrates (1.8g fiber, 3.5g sugar) | 3.6g protein

CHOCOLATE & GRANOLA APPLE NACHOS

prep time: 10 minutes ♥ yields: 2 servings

In most of my childhood brown bag lunches, my dad added apple slices as a healthy side for my plain peanut butter sandwich. That tradition carried on throughout high school too, and when I left for college and lived in the dorm suites, I forgot a small knife and cutting board my first quarter and had to eat my apples whole. Because they didn't quite taste the same like that, I remembered to pack the necessary kitchen knife and cutting board as I left home at the end of winter break. Back in our suite, my roommates and I enjoyed sliced apples quite often the following quarter, and we started to dress them up with toppings like drizzled peanut butter and chocolate chips—our own version of apple "nachos." These are a slightly healthier version, although just as chocolaty as the ones from college!

for the granola
½ tsp maple syrup
½ tsp water
2 tbsp (6g) old-fashioned oats
1 tbsp (2g) brown rice cereal

for the chocolate sauce
2 tsp unsweetened cocoa powder
½ tsp maple syrup
1 tsp nonfat milk
1 medium apple, thinly sliced

1. To prepare the granola, stir together the maple syrup, water, oats, and brown rice cereal in a small microwave-safe ramekin. Microwave on 30% power for 1 minute. Stir, making sure to scrape up any pieces stuck to the bottom. Microwave on 30% power for an additional 1 minute or until crunchy. Let the granola cool completely to room temperature in the ramekin.
2. To prepare the chocolate sauce, stir together the cocoa powder, maple syrup, and milk in a small bowl.
3. Arrange the apple slices on a plate. Sprinkle with the granola, and drizzle with the chocolate sauce.

C

Nutrition Information: 71 calories | 0.7g fat (0g saturated fat, 0.3g unsaturated fat) | 0.1mg cholesterol
28.0mg sodium | 16.3g carbohydrates (2.8g fiber, 9.4g sugar) | 1.3g protein

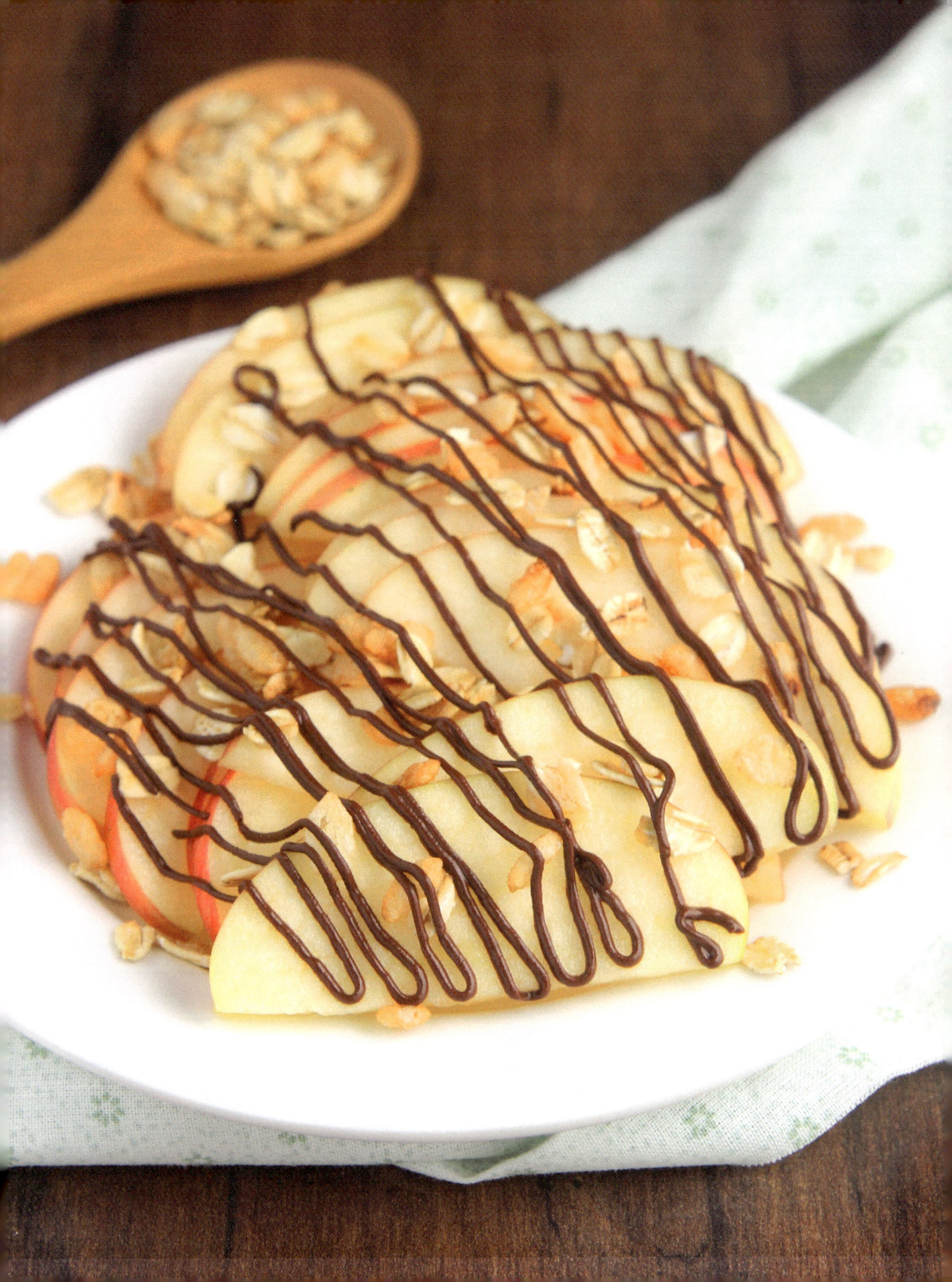

DESSERTS

♥ ♥ ♥

Dessert has always been my favorite meal of the day. As a little girl, I found a small treat in my lunchbox every day, usually a store-bought chocolate chip cookie or cream-filled chocolate cupcake. After dinner, our parents allowed my brother and me to peek into the pantry for another dessert, often similar to what we nibbled on earlier at school. That sweet tooth accompanied me throughout childhood, college, and clear through to today. As a result, this is the biggest chapter and full of my favorite chocolate desserts!

CHOCOLATE CHIP COOKIES

prep time: 20 minutes ♥ inactive time: 30 minutes
baking time: 9-11 minutes ♥ yields: 24 cookies

Between working part-time and shuttling my brother and me to school, sports practices, and music lessons, Mom hardly ever had time to cook dinner, let alone bake treats for us. On the rare occasion that she pulled out her big metal mixing bowl and electric beaters, Mom usually whipped up a batch of classic chocolate chip cookies using the recipe on the back of the iconic yellow bag of chocolate chips. After popping the trays in the oven, she always handed over that metal mixing bowl to us so we could eat the extra cookie dough. I'd draw a line down the middle with my finger, and my brother and I each took a half, using spoons to scrape up every last morsel. I still think of those childhood days every time I bake chocolate chip cookies, even when they're my healthier version and I don't have to share the bowl with anyone else!

2 cups (240g) all-purpose flour
2 tsp cornstarch
1 ½ tsp baking powder
½ tsp salt
¼ cup (56g) unsalted butter, melted and cooled slightly
2 large eggs, room temperature
1 tbsp (15mL) vanilla extract
1 cup (212g) light brown sugar
¼ cup (56g) semisweet chocolate chips
2 tbsp (28g) miniature chocolate chips

1. Whisk together the flour, cornstarch, baking powder, and salt in a medium bowl. In a separate bowl, whisk together the butter, eggs, and vanilla. Stir in the brown sugar, smearing out any clumps along the side of the bowl. Add the flour mixture, stirring until just incorporated. Fold in the semisweet chocolate chips and 1 tablespoon of miniature chocolate chips. Chill the cookie dough for at least 30 minutes.

2. Preheat the oven to 375°F, and line two baking sheets with silicone baking mats or parchment paper.

3. Drop the cookie dough into rounded scoops onto the prepared baking sheets, and gently press the remaining miniature chocolate chips on top. Bake at 375°F for 9-11 minutes. Cool the cookies on the baking sheets for 10 minutes before transferring to wire racks.

AMY'S ADVICE
For thicker cookies, chill the dough for at least 2 hours before baking!

Nutrition Information: 114 calories | 3.4g fat (1.9g saturated fat, 0.9g unsaturated fat) | 20.7mg cholesterol
88.9mg sodium | 22.4g carbohydrates (0.3g fiber, 13.9g sugar) | 1.6g protein

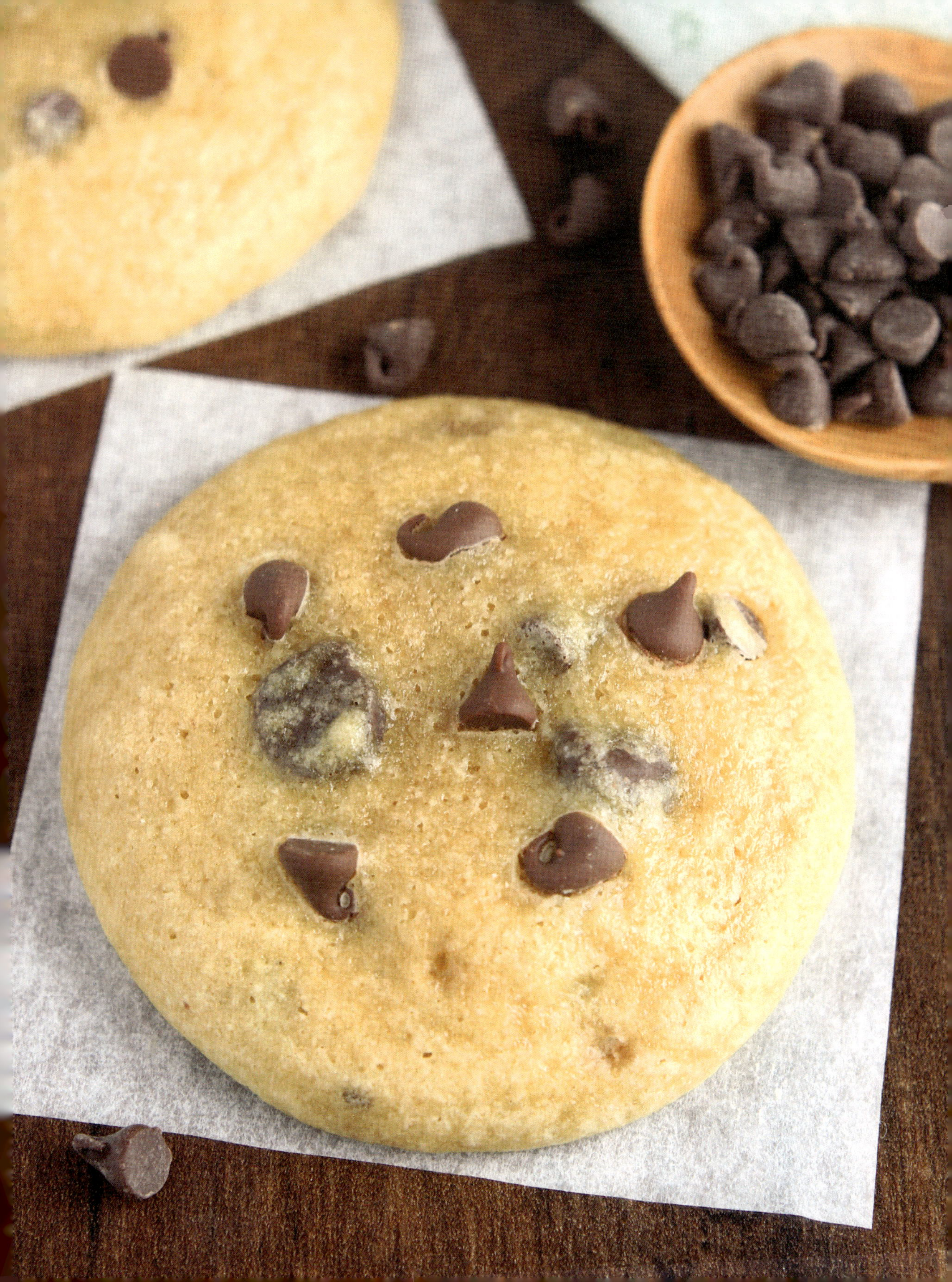

DOUBLE CHOCOLATE CHIP COOKIES

prep time: 20 minutes ♥ baking time: 9-11 minutes ♥ yields: 24 cookies

Since my mom only occasionally baked, she usually bought treats from the store to slip inside our lunch boxes alongside our apple slices and peanut butter sandwiches. One week, she brought home a package of double chocolate chip cookies from the supermarket, and that marked the first time my brother and I ate cookies made with chocolate dough. I immediately fell in love with their fudgy brownie-like texture, and I began requesting those over the regular chocolate chip cookies she generally bought. These are my healthier homemade version, which contain even more chocolate than those original packaged cookies!

- 1 ¼ cups (150g) all-purpose flour
- ½ cup (40g) unsweetened cocoa powder
- ½ tsp baking powder
- ¼ tsp salt
- ¼ cup (56g) unsalted butter, melted and cooled slightly
- 2 large eggs, room temperature
- 1 tbsp (15mL) vanilla extract
- 1 cup (212g) light brown sugar
- ¼ cup (56) dark chocolate chips
- 2 tbsp (28g) miniature chocolate chips

1. Preheat the oven to 350°F, and line two baking sheets with silicone baking mats or parchment paper.
2. Whisk together the flour, cocoa powder, baking powder, and salt in a medium bowl. In a separate bowl, whisk together the butter, eggs, and vanilla. Stir in the brown sugar, smearing out any clumps along the side of the bowl. Add the flour mixture, stirring until just incorporated. Fold in the dark chocolate chips and 1 tablespoon of miniature chocolate chips.
3. Drop the dough into 24 rounded scoops on the prepared baking sheets, flatten to about half of their height using a spatula, and gently press the remaining miniature chocolate chips into the tops. Bake at 350°F for 9-11 minutes. Cool the cookies on the baking sheets for 10 minutes before transferring to wire racks.

AMY'S ADVICE
Try regular semisweet chocolate chips instead of dark chocolate chips for a slightly lighter taste.

Nutrition Information: 102 calories | 3.6g fat (2.0g saturated fat, 0.9g unsaturated fat) | 20.7mg cholesterol
66.8mg sodium | 20.1g carbohydrates (1.0g fiber, 13.7g sugar) | 1.6g protein

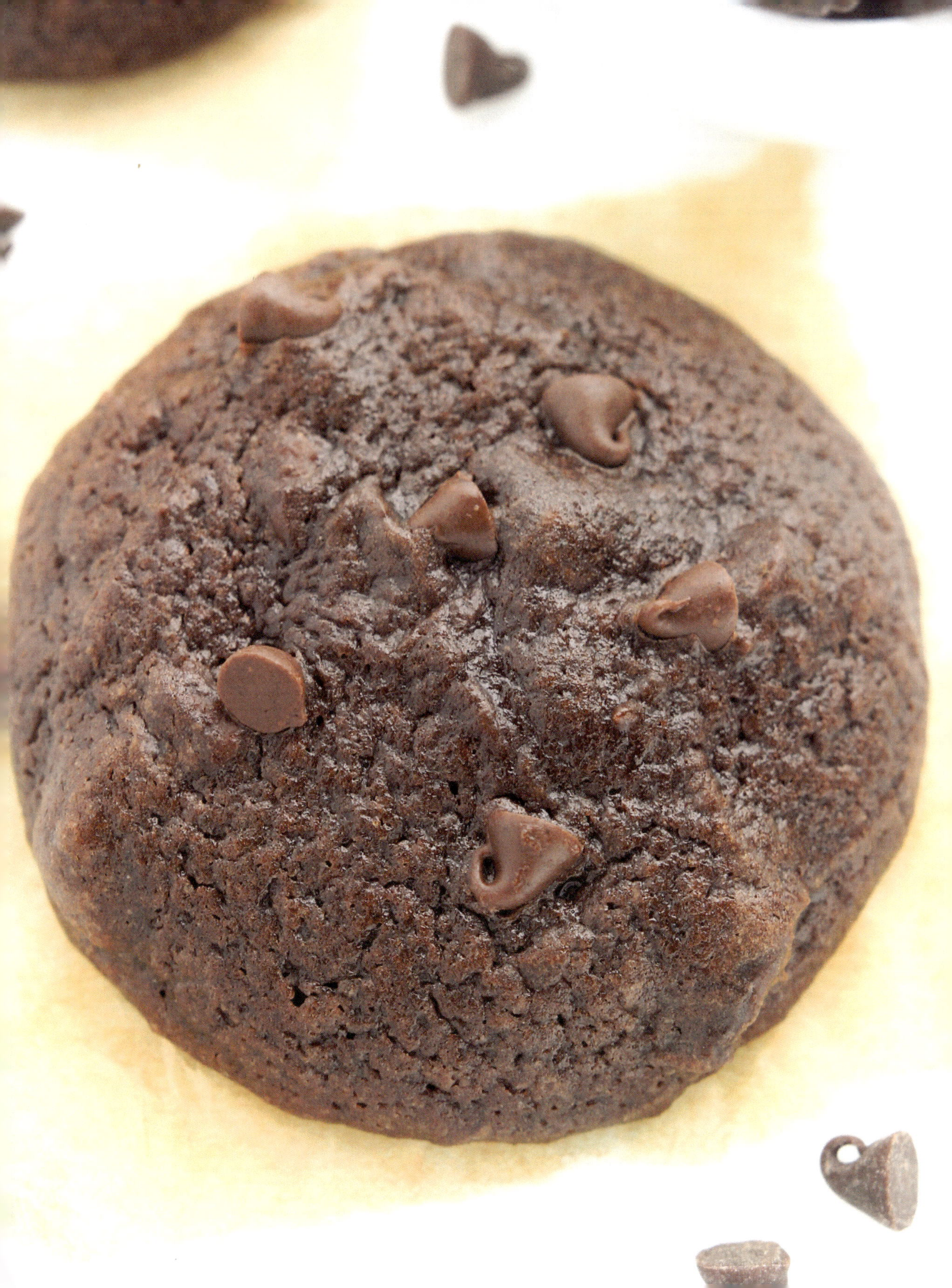

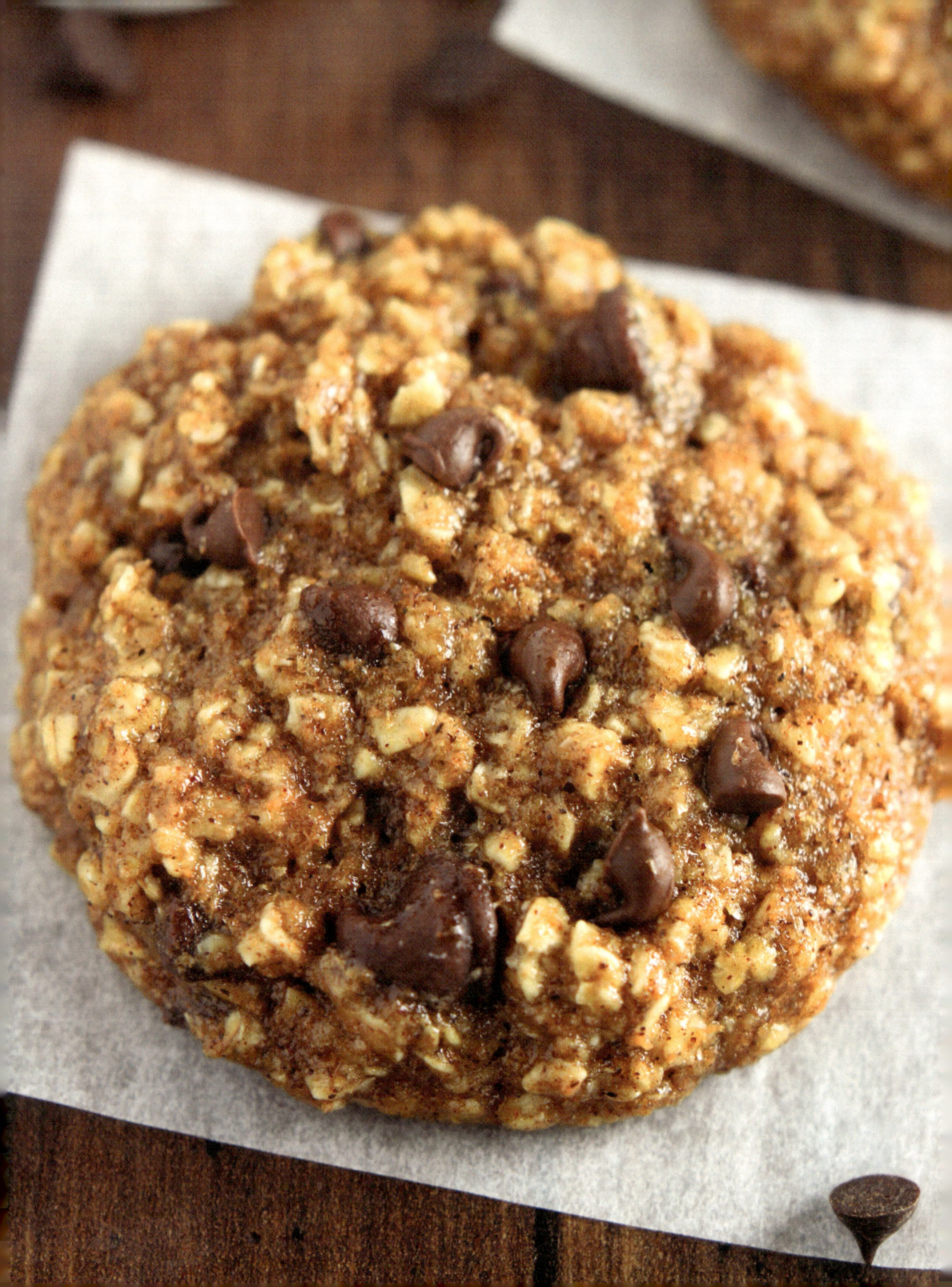

OATMEAL CHOCOLATE CHIP COOKIES

prep time: 20 minutes ♥ inactive time: 30 minutes
baking time: 13-15 minutes ♥ yields: 15 cookies

My mom stored recipes clipped from magazines and newspapers in a small photo album on her cookbook shelf, including one for oatmeal chocolate chip cookies. While she worked part-time during the summers, my younger brother and I would flip to that recipe, mix up the cookie dough, and pop the bowl into the refrigerator until she arrived home. (We weren't allowed to use the oven!) This recipe is my chewier—and much healthier—version of those irresistible cookies.

1 cup (100g) instant oats
¾ cup (90g) whole wheat flour
1 ½ tsp baking powder
1 ½ tsp ground cinnamon
¼ tsp salt
2 tbsp (28g) unsalted butter, melted and cooled slightly
1 large egg, room temperature
1 tsp vanilla extract
½ cup (120mL) agave
2 ½ tbsp (35g) dark chocolate chips
1 ½ tbsp (21g) miniature chocolate chips

1. Whisk together the oats, flour, baking powder, cinnamon, and salt in a medium bowl. In a separate bowl, whisk together the butter, egg, and vanilla. Stir in the agave. Add the oat mixture, stirring until just incorporated. Fold in the dark chocolate chips and 1 tablespoon of miniature chocolate chips. Chill the dough for 30 minutes.
2. Preheat the oven to 325°F, and line a baking sheet with a silicone baking mat or parchment paper.
3. Drop the dough into 15 rounded scoops onto the prepared baking sheet, and gently press the remaining miniature chocolate chips into the tops. Bake at 325°F for 13-15 minutes. Cool the cookies on the baking sheet for 10 minutes before transferring to a wire rack.

AMY'S ADVICE
Visit my website for more oatmeal cookie flavor variations, like carrot cake and apple pie. They're some of the most popular recipes on my blog!

C   DF

Nutrition Information: 102 calories | 2.5g fat (1.2g saturated fat, 0.6g unsaturated fat) | 13.9mg cholesterol 93.2mg sodium | 19.3g carbohydrates (1.6g fiber, 10.7g sugar) | 1.9g protein

FROSTED RED VELVET COOKIES

prep time: 20 minutes ♥ inactive time: 2 hours
baking time: 10-12 minutes ♥ yields: 24 cookies

I tasted my first piece of red velvet cake when I was 20 years old, and I was immediately infatuated with its complex flavor: not quite vanilla, not quite chocolate, yet somehow both at the same time. Paired with sweet cream cheese frosting, that slice of cake disappeared embarrassingly quickly! These cookies have the same iconic flavors but require much less time to bake and assemble, making them perfect for satisfying red velvet cravings in a flash.

for the cookies
1 ¾ cups (210g) all-purpose flour
½ cup (40g) unsweetened cocoa powder
1 ½ tsp cornstarch
1 tsp baking powder
½ tsp salt
¼ cup (56g) unsalted butter, melted and cooled slightly
2 large eggs, room temperature
2 tsp vanilla extract
1 cup (212g) light brown sugar
3 ½ tsp red food coloring

for the frosting
½ cup (120g) plain nonfat Greek yogurt
4 oz (113g) block-style fat-free cream cheese
1 serving (7g) fat-free, sugar-free instant cheesecake pudding mix
2 tbsp (27g) Truvia®

1. Preheat the oven to 350°F, and line two baking sheets with silicone baking mats or parchment paper.

2. To prepare the cookies, whisk together the flour, cocoa powder, cornstarch, baking powder, and salt in a medium bowl. In a separate bowl, whisk together the butter, eggs, and vanilla. Stir in the brown sugar, smearing out any clumps along the side of the bowl. Carefully stir in the red food coloring. Add the flour mixture, stirring until just incorporated.

3. Drop the cookie dough into 12 rounded scoops onto the prepared baking sheet, and flatten them to about half their height using a spatula. Bake at 350°F for 10-12 minutes. Cool the cookies on the baking sheets for 5 minutes before transferring to a wire rack to cool completely.

4. While the cookies bake, prepare the frosting. Beat the Greek yogurt, cream cheese, pudding mix, and Truvia® in a medium bowl on low speed for 2 minutes or until thick. Chill for at least 2 hours before spreading on top of the cooled cookies.

AMY'S ADVICE
On the baking aisle, there should be large bottles of red food coloring sold individually. Don't use the tiny dropper bottles; they don't contain enough food coloring. Be careful when adding the food coloring because it stains clothes easily!

Nutrition Information: 103 calories | 2.6g fat (1.3g saturated fat, 0.9g unsaturated fat) | 21.5mg cholesterol 147.1mg sodium | 20.8g carbohydrates (0.9g fiber, 12.2g sugar) | 3.0g protein

FUDGY DARK CHOCOLATE BROWNIES

prep time: 20 minutes ♥ baking time: 15-17 minutes
inactive time: 3 hours ♥ yields: 16 brownies

Growing up, I believed that all brownies came from boxed mixes. It was the only way my mom ever baked them, and she always kept the pantry well stocked with the fudgiest varieties. When I reached high school, she explained that it was because she accidentally made "scrambled egg brownies" for a bake sale as a seven-year-old by adding the hot melted chocolate to the egg mixture too quickly! This healthier version avoids that problem by exclusively using cocoa powder for the chocolate component, and as a result, these homemade brownies are some of the darkest, richest, and fudgiest that I've ever tasted.

¾ cup (90g) white whole wheat flour
¾ cup (60g) unsweetened cocoa powder
¼ tsp baking powder
¼ tsp salt
1 ½ tbsp (21g) unsalted butter, melted and cooled slightly
1 large egg, room temperature
1 tsp vanilla extract
⅓ cup (80g) plain nonfat Greek yogurt
½ cup (120mL) maple syrup
¼ cup (56g) chopped dark chocolate, divided

1. Preheat the oven to 300°F, and lightly coat an 8"-square pan with nonstick cooking spray.
2. Whisk together the flour, cocoa powder, baking powder, and salt in a medium bowl. In a separate bowl, whisk together the butter, egg, and vanilla. Stir in the Greek yogurt, mixing until no large lumps remain. Stir in the maple syrup. Add the flour mixture, stirring until just incorporated. Fold in 3 tablespoons of the chopped dark chocolate.
3. Spread the batter into the prepared pan, and gently press the remaining chopped dark chocolate into the top. Bake at 300°F for 15-17 minutes. Cool completely to room temperature in the pan. Let the brownies set for at least 3 additional hours before slicing for the fudgiest texture.

AMY'S ADVICE
For a really decadent treat, top these brownies with the dark chocolate frosting on P.117!

C

Nutrition Information: 92 calories | 3.6g fat (1.5g saturated fat, 0.5g unsaturated fat) | 25.9mg cholesterol
147.8mg sodium | 13.6g carbohydrates (2.3g fiber, 6.3g sugar) | 3.6g protein

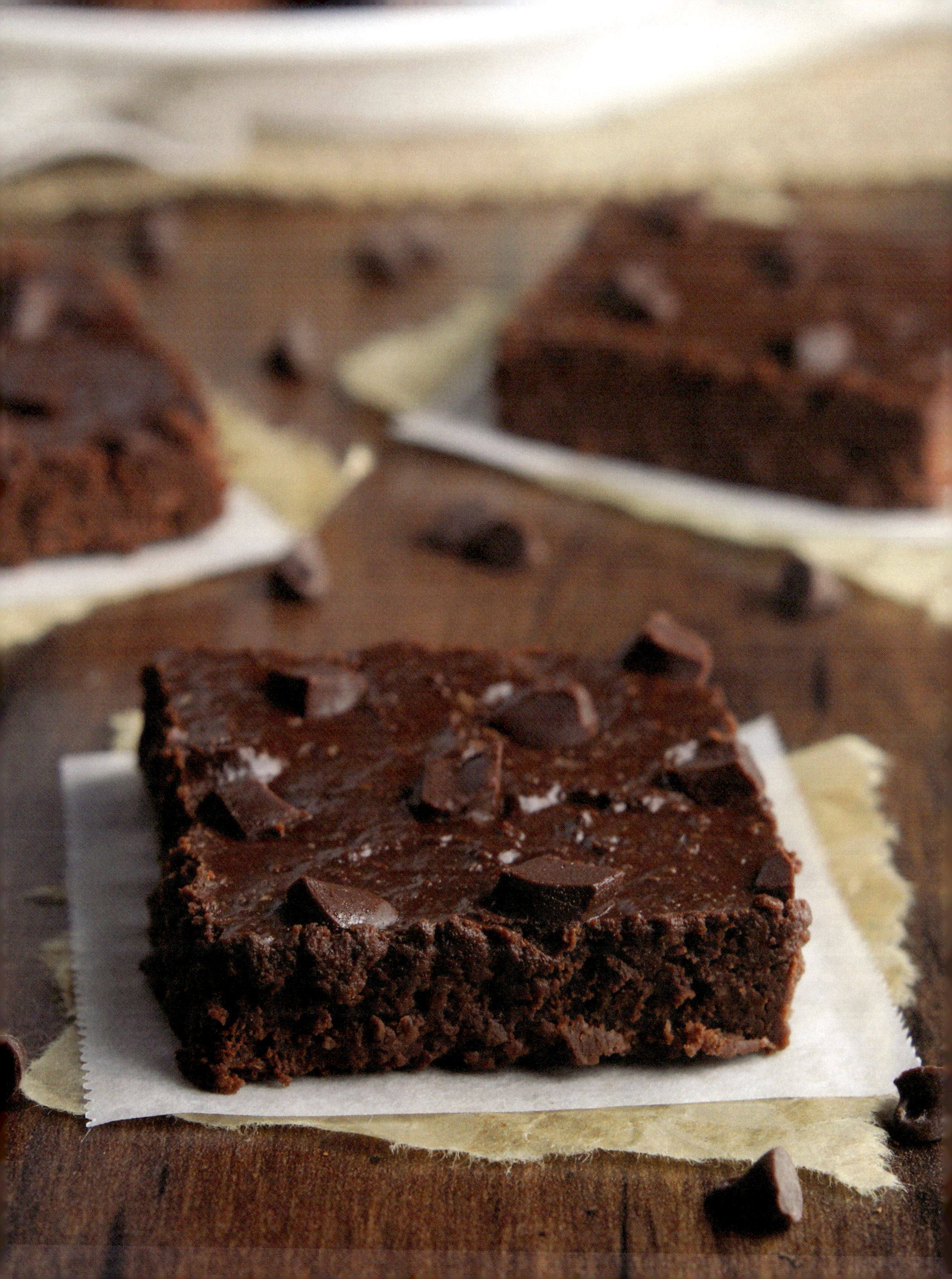

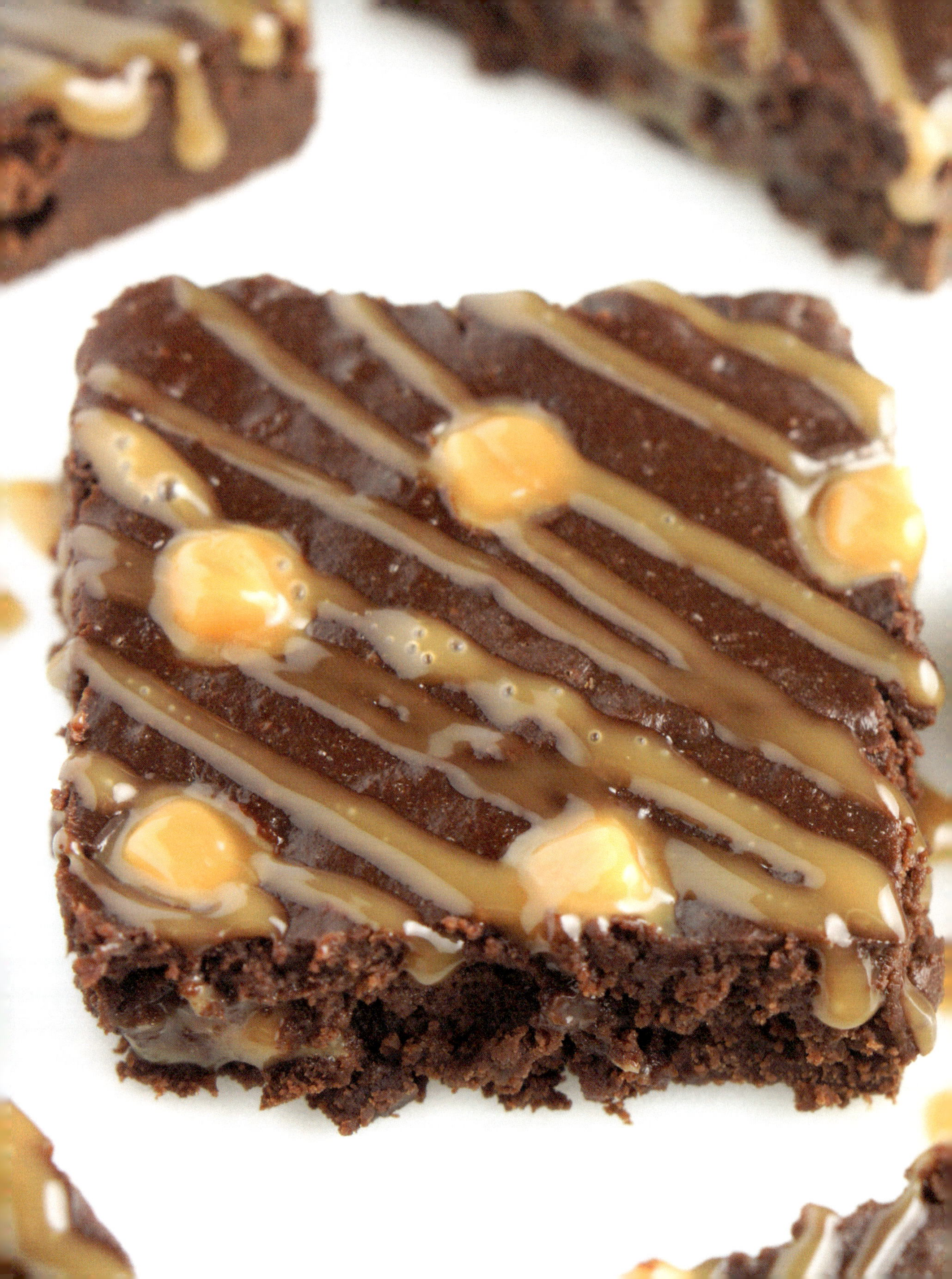

FUDGY CARAMEL BROWNIES

prep time: 20 minutes ♥ baking time: 17-20 minutes
inactive time: 3 hours ♥ yields: 16 brownies

The birthday of one of my close friends falls on the day before mine, so during my high school years, we celebrated every year by going out to dinner at a well-known restaurant chain and ordering their version of a brownie sundae for dessert. The warm, fudgy brownie came topped with vanilla ice cream, and we always asked for extra chocolate and caramel sauce. Because birthdays fall just once a year, I created an easier everyday dessert with our favorite components from that special celebratory treat: these caramel-filled brownies.

- ¾ cup (90g) all-purpose flour
- ¾ cup (60g) unsweetened cocoa powder
- ¼ tsp baking powder
- ¼ tsp salt
- 2 tbsp (28g) unsalted butter, melted and cooled slightly
- 2 large eggs, room temperature
- 1 tsp vanilla extract
- ½ cup (96g) granulated sugar
- ¼ cup (60g) plain nonfat Greek yogurt
- ¼ cup (60mL) nonfat milk
- 10 caramel candy squares, diced (such as Kraft®)
- 2 tbsp (30mL) caramel sauce

1. Preheat the oven to 300°F, and lightly coat an 8"-square pan with nonstick cooking spray.
2. Whisk together the flour, cocoa powder, baking powder, and salt in a medium bowl. In a separate bowl, whisk together the butter, eggs, and vanilla. Mix in the sugar and Greek yogurt, stirring until no large lumps remain. Mix in the milk. Add the flour mixture, stirring until just incorporated. Fold in ⅔ of the diced caramel candies.
3. Spread the batter into the prepared pan, and press the remaining diced caramel candies into the top. Bake at 300°F for 17-20 minutes. Cool completely to room temperature in the pan. Let the brownies set for at least 3 additional hours before slicing for the fudgiest texture. Just before serving, drizzle with the caramel sauce.

AMY'S ADVICE
Top these brownies with a small scoop of vanilla ice cream for an extra sweet treat!

Nutrition Information: 105 calories | 2.9g fat (1.4g saturated fat, 1.0g unsaturated fat) | 27.2mg cholesterol
125.8mg sodium | 18.8g carbohydrates (1.7g fiber, 11.2g sugar) | 3.0g protein

CARAMEL SEVEN LAYER BARS

prep time: 20 minutes ♥ baking time: 18-20 minutes
inactive time: 3 hours ♥ yields: 16 bars

I had never heard of seven layer bars (also called magic bars) until I started blogging, but after my first two years, recipes for them began popping up everywhere I looked. Traditional versions include—you guessed it!—seven ingredients: graham crackers, butter, coconut, chocolate chips, nuts, butterscotch, and sweetened condensed milk. That makes for one delicious treat—and a whole lot of calories! Eventually I created this lighter version, and one of my close friends called them even better than the originals. They disappeared in the blink of an eye!

- 10 full sheets (155g) honey graham crackers
- 3 large egg whites, room temperature
- 6 tbsp (30g) reduced fat unsweetened shredded coconut
- ¼ cup (56g) miniature chocolate chips
- ¼ cup (30g) finely chopped pecans
- 4 caramel candy squares, diced (such as Kraft®)
- 4 oz (113g) fat-free sweetened condensed milk
- ¼ cup (60g) plain nonfat Greek yogurt
- 1 tbsp (13g) Truvia®

1. Preheat the oven to 350°F, and coat a 9"-square pan with nonstick cooking spray.
2. Break the graham crackers into pieces, and add to a food processor or blender. Pulse until they're fine crumbs. Transfer the crumbs to a bowl, and mix in the egg whites until fully incorporated. Press the mixture into the bottom of the prepared pan.
3. Sprinkle the coconut, miniature chocolate chips, pecans, and diced caramel candy over the graham cracker crust in the order listed. In a small bowl, stir together the sweetened condensed milk, Greek yogurt, and Truvia®. Evenly drizzle the milk mixture over the toppings.
4. Bake at 350°F for 18-20 minutes. Cool completely to room temperature, and allow the bars to set for at least 3 additional hours before slicing into squares.

AMY'S ADVICE
Substitute walnuts or cashews for a different nutty flavor!

Nutrition Information: 99 calories | 4.0g fat (1.3g saturated fat, 1.7g unsaturated fat) | 0.2mg cholesterol 79.7mg sodium | 13.8g carbohydrates (0.7g fiber, 7.8g sugar) | 2.2g protein

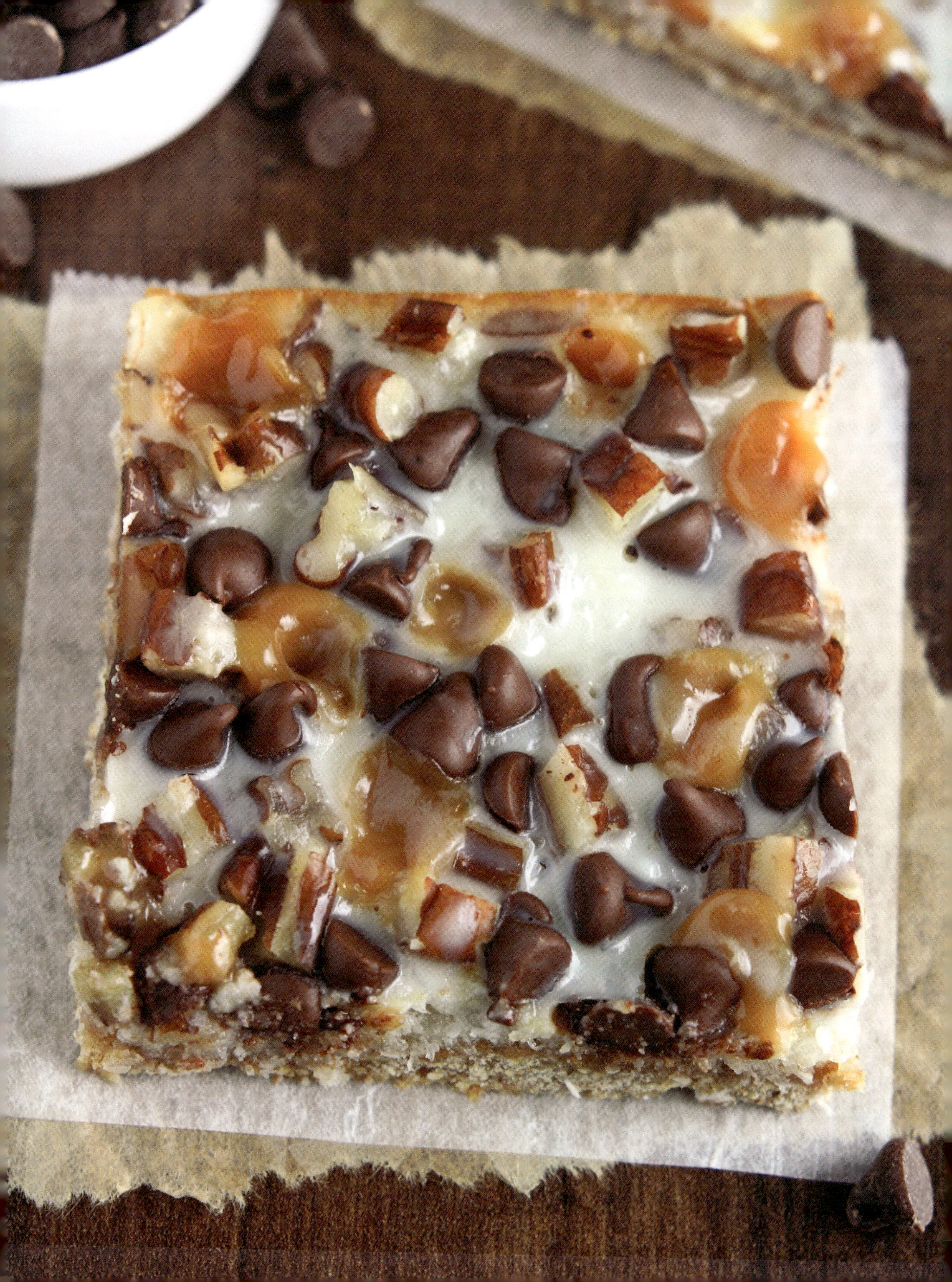

STRAWBERRY FROSTED CHOCOLATE CEREAL TREATS

prep time: 20 minutes ♥ inactive time: 2 hours ♥ yields: 16 bars

Marshmallow cereal treats are one of the only desserts my guy will eat, so I make a batch for him on nearly every birthday and Valentine's Day in fun cookie-cutter shapes. Because he prefers his extremely chewy and gooey, I always add a secret ingredient: extra marshmallows!

for the frosting
- 1 cup (140g) frozen unsweetened strawberries, thawed
- 1 ½ cups (360g) plain nonfat Greek yogurt
- 2 servings (14g) fat-free, sugar-free instant vanilla pudding mix
- ¼ cup (6g) granulated sucralose

for the treats
- 4 ½ cups (174g) chocolate rice cereal (such as Cocoa Pebbles®)
- 1 ½ tbsp (21g) unsalted butter
- 3 ¾ cups (170g) miniature marshmallows

1. To prepare the frosting, purée the strawberries, and add the purée to a small pot. Cook over medium-low heat, stirring frequently, for 4-6 minutes or until the mixture has reduced by half. Cool completely to room temperature.

2. Add the strawberry purée, Greek yogurt, pudding mix, and sucralose to a large bowl. Beat on low speed for 2 minutes or until thickened. Chill for 2 hours.

3. To prepare the treats, lightly coat a 9"-square pan with nonstick cooking spray. Add the cereal to a large bowl. Add the butter to a large saucepan, and melt over medium-low heat. Add the marshmallows, and cook, stirring constantly, until they appear to have fully melted. Pour the marshmallow mixture over the cereal, and stir until the cereal is completely coated.

4. Transfer the cereal mixture to the prepared pan. Coat your hands with cooking spray, and gently press the mixture evenly into the pan. Cool completely to room temperature before frosting and slicing into squares.

AMY'S ADVICE
These are best if eaten the same day they're assembled. The frosting will stay fresh for at least 3 days if covered and chilled. The cereal treats will stay fresh for at least 1 day if stored in an airtight container.

GF

Nutrition Information: 110 calories | 1.6g fat (1.1g saturated fat, 0.3g unsaturated fat) | 2.9mg cholesterol | 117.1mg sodium | 21.5g carbohydrates (0.4g fiber, 12.8g sugar) | 2.8g protein

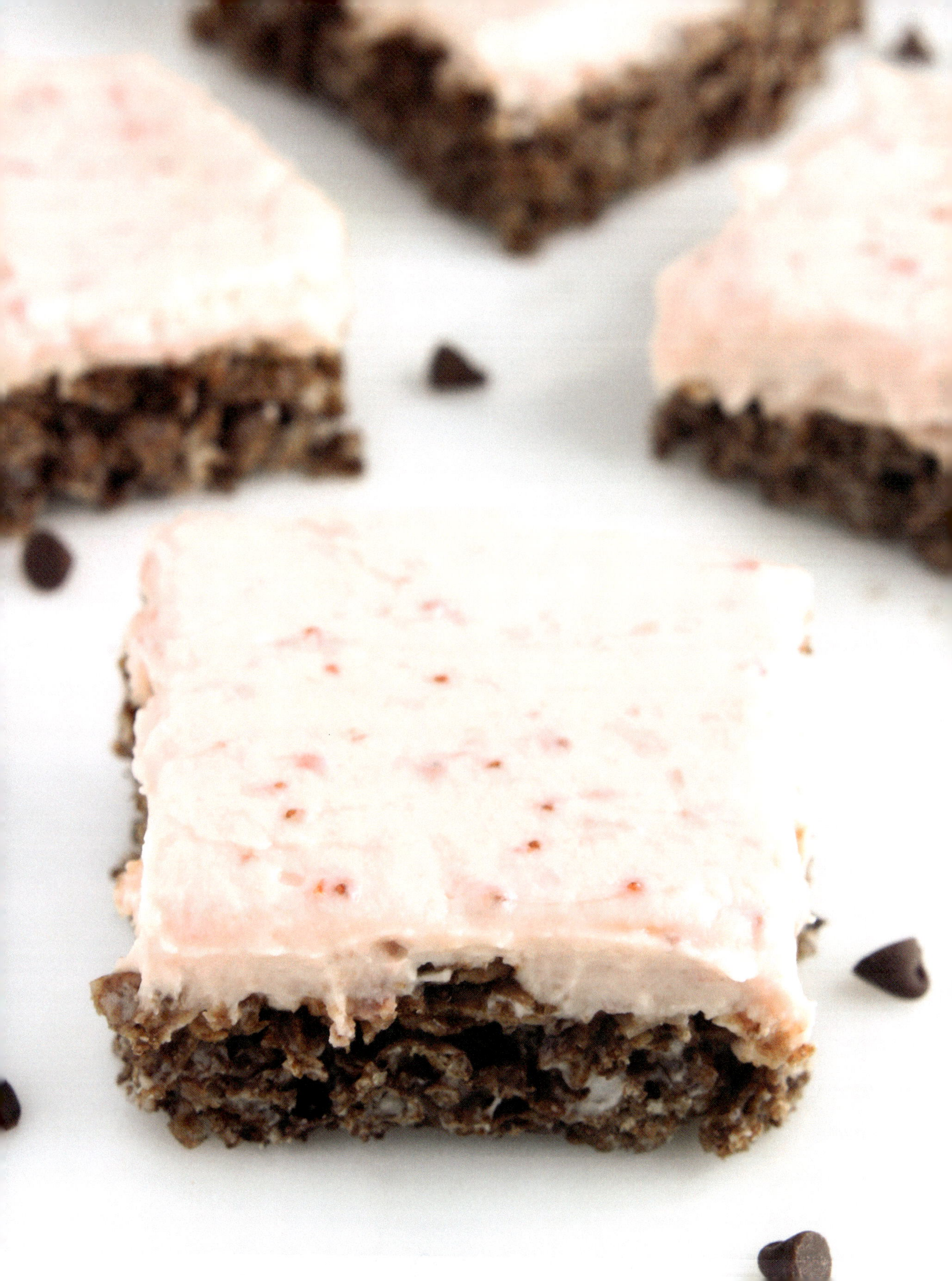

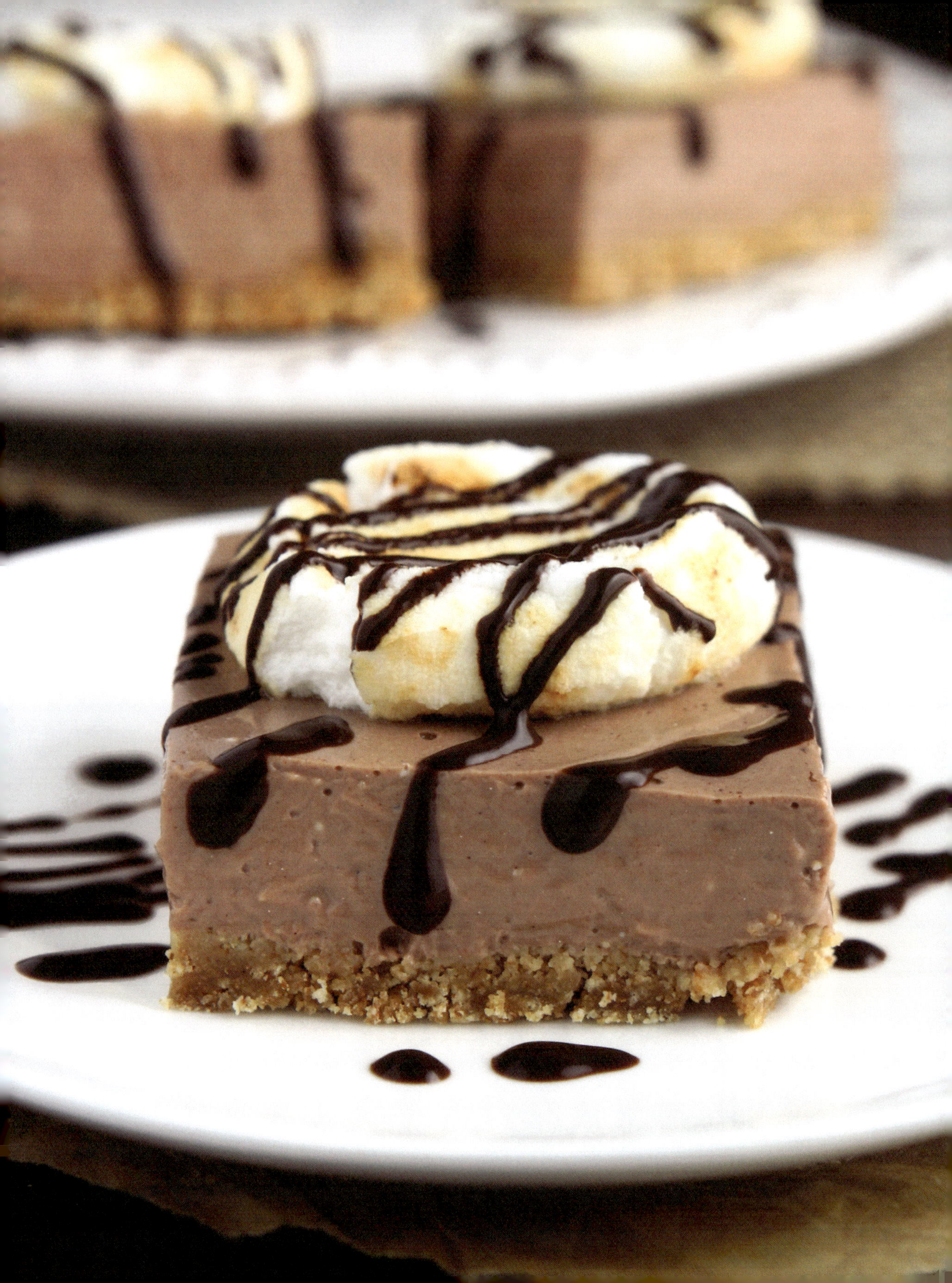

S'MORES CHEESECAKE BARS

prep time: 25 minutes ♥ baking time: 26-29 minutes
inactive time: 3 hours ♥ yields: 16 bars

Growing up, my family went camping in the mountains at least twice each summer. We spent the days hiking and swimming, and we slept in a tent, or sometimes under the stars, in warm sleeping bags on thin inflatable mattresses. Nearly every night before bed, my mom would pull out marshmallows for us to toast, along with graham crackers and chocolate bars to make s'mores. I rarely camp anymore because I now prefer daily showers, so these cheesecake bars are how I get my s'mores fix!

for the crust
7 full sheets (109g) honey graham crackers
1 tbsp (14g) unsalted butter, melted and cooled slightly
1 large egg white, room temperature
1 tbsp (15mL) nonfat milk, room temperature

for the filling
2 (8oz) blocks fat-free cream cheese, room temperature
½ cup (96g) granulated sugar
1 large egg white, room temperature
¼ cup (20g) unsweetened cocoa powder
1 tsp cornstarch
2 tsp vanilla extract

for topping
8 regular marshmallows, sliced in half
2 tbsp (30mL) chocolate syrup

1. Preheat the oven to 300°F, and lightly coat an 8"-square pan with nonstick cooking spray.
2. Add the graham crackers to a food processor or blender, and pulse until they're fine crumbs. Pour the crumbs into a bowl, and add the butter, egg white, and milk. Stir until everything is thoroughly combined. Press the mixture into the bottom of the prepared pan. Bake at 300°F for 6 minutes. Cool completely.
3. Beat the cream cheese and sugar in a large bowl until the mixture is creamy. Add the egg white, beating until incorporated. Mix in the cocoa powder, cornstarch, and vanilla. Pour the filling on top of the cooled crust.
4. Bake at 300°F for 20-23 minutes or until the center only jiggles slightly. Cool completely to room temperature. Cover the top with plastic wrap, ensuring that the plastic completely touches the top of the cheesecake, and chill for at least 3 hours before slicing and serving.
5. To serve, lightly toast the marshmallow halves with a culinary torch or long-nosed lighter. Immediately place a toasted marshmallow on top of each cheesecake square, and drizzle with the chocolate syrup.

HP

Nutrition Information: 113 calories | 1.5g fat (0.6g saturated fat, 0.6g unsaturated fat) | 7.0mg cholesterol 259.1mg sodium | 19.0g carbohydrates (0.7g fiber, 12.5g sugar) | 5.3g protein

DARK CHOCOLATE RASPBERRY TRUFFLES

prep time: 20 minutes ♥ inactive time: 2 hours ♥ yields: 16 truffles

During college, I discovered a small gourmet chocolate shop located on the very edge of downtown. It was owned and operated by a very sweet and generous man, and he added at least one jelly-filled truffle of your choice "on the house" to every purchase. Because neither my wallet nor waistline could afford daily trips there, I started making my own healthier version at home, complete with a fresh fruit center instead.

1 cup (80g) unsweetened cocoa powder
½ cup (120g) unsweetened applesauce
3 tbsp (45mL) honey
¼ tsp vanilla extract
16 large raspberries, washed and dried

1. Mix together the cocoa powder, applesauce, honey, and vanilla in a medium bowl until smooth. Place the bowl in the refrigerator and chill for at least 2 hours or up to 1 day.
2. Divide the chocolate mixture into 16 pieces. Working with one piece at a time, roll into a ball; then flatten into a circle. Place a raspberry into the center, and fold the chocolate up around the sides. Roll back into a ball, and place the truffle onto a sheet of wax paper. Repeat with the remaining chocolate and raspberries. Chill until ready to serve.

AMY'S ADVICE
If the chocolate mixture sticks too much to your hands while rolling into balls, moisten your palms with a few drops of water. The moisture won't completely prevent the chocolate from sticking to your palms, but it'll at least reduce the amount of leftover chocolate!

C   GF   DF   P

Nutrition Information: 26 calories | 0.5g fat (0.0g saturated fat, 0.0g unsaturated fat) | 0.0mg cholesterol | 65.3mg sodium | 7.3g carbohydrates (2.2g fiber, 4.0g sugar) | 1.0g protein

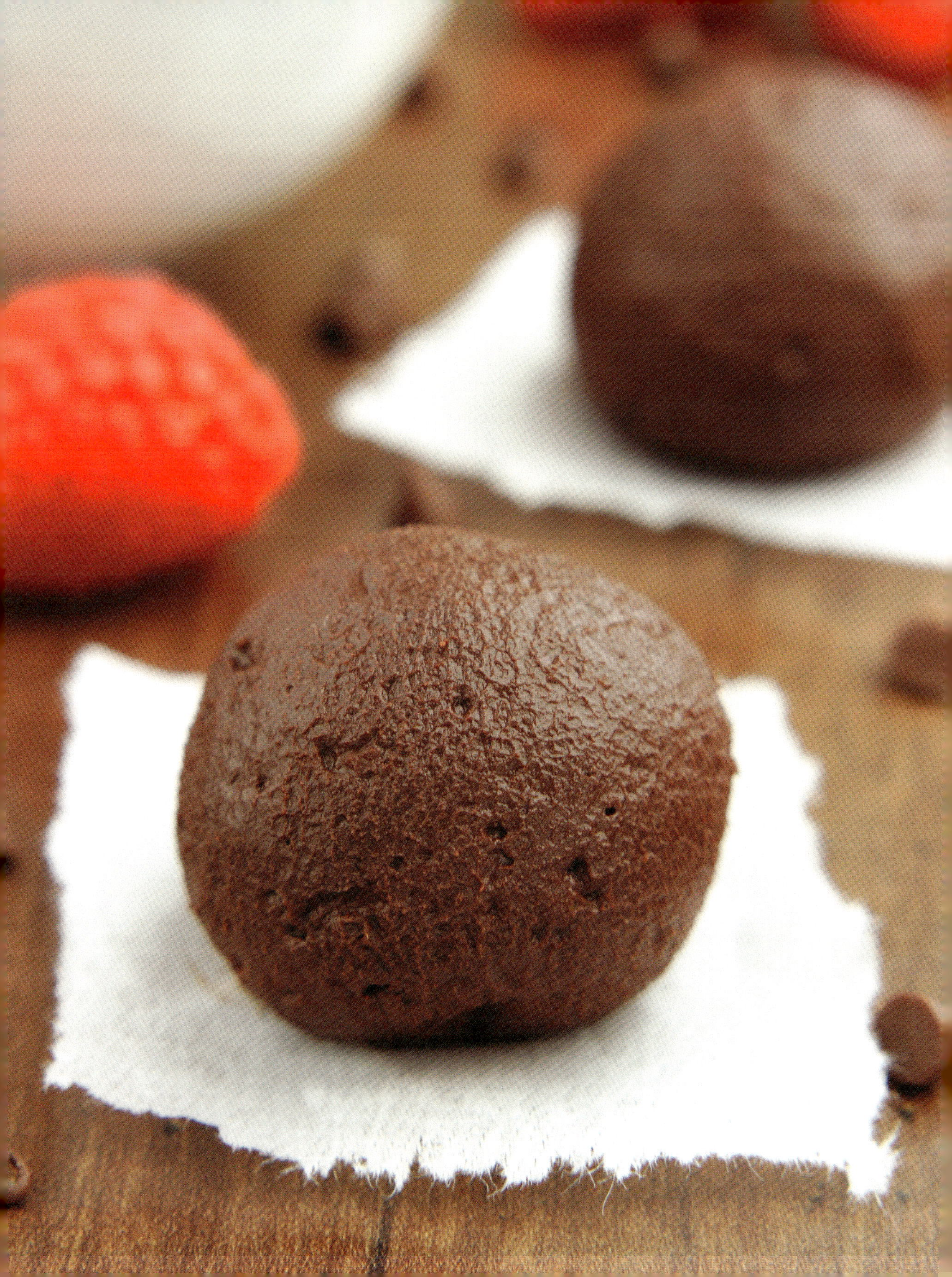

PEPPERMINT HOT CHOCOLATE TRUFFLES

prep time: 20 minutes ♥ inactive time: 2 hours ♥ yields: 16 truffles

During the holiday season, my mom loves to stop by the coffee shop down the street on the weekends for a small peppermint hot chocolate as an afternoon pick-me-up. While she was out running errands one Saturday, I created this truffle version of her holiday drink for her to pair with the steaming mug when she came home, and it was nearly impossible to determine which she enjoyed more!

- 1 cup (80g) unsweetened cocoa powder
- ½ cup (120g) unsweetened applesauce
- 3 tbsp (45mL) honey
- ¼ tsp peppermint extract
- 16 miniature marshmallows

1. Mix together the cocoa powder, applesauce, honey, and peppermint extract in a medium bowl until smooth. Place the bowl in the refrigerator and chill for at least 2 hours or up to 1 day.
2. Divide the chocolate mixture into 16 pieces. Working with one piece at a time, roll into a ball; then flatten into a circle. Place a marshmallow into the center, and fold the chocolate up around the sides. Roll back into a ball, and place the truffle onto a sheet of wax paper. Repeat with the remaining chocolate and marshmallows. Chill until ready to serve.

AMY'S ADVICE
If the chocolate mixture sticks too much to your hands while rolling into balls, moisten your palms with a few drops of water. The moisture won't completely prevent the chocolate from sticking to your palms, but it'll at least reduce the amount of leftover chocolate!

GF DF

Nutrition Information: 27 calories | 0.5g fat (0.0g saturated fat, 0.0g unsaturated fat) | 0.0mg cholesterol 65.9mg sodium | 7.7g carbohydrates (2.1g fiber, 4.4g sugar) | 1.0g protein

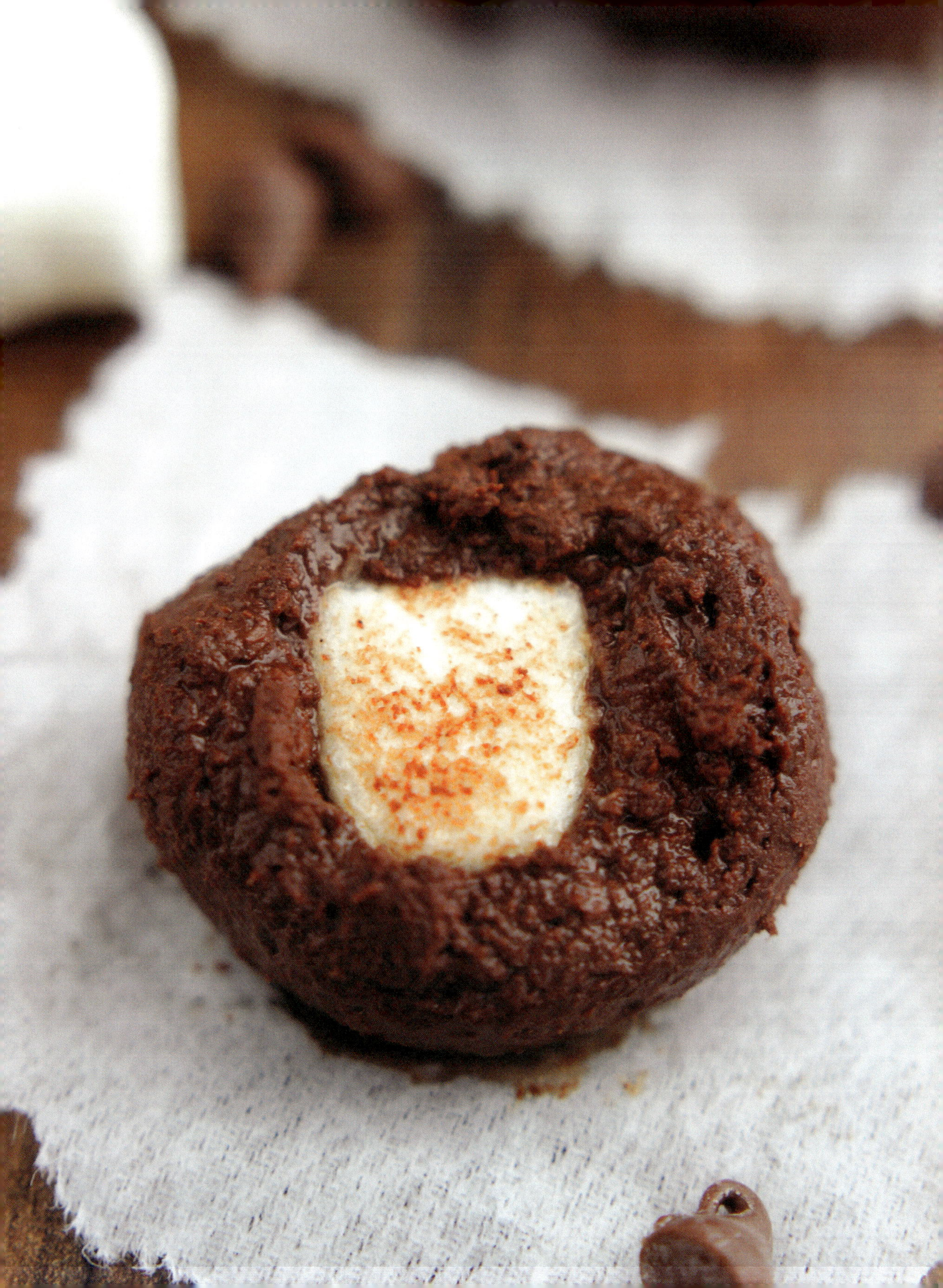

MINI WHITE CHOCOLATE BERRY LEMON PARFAITS

prep time: 10 minutes ♥ inactive time: 2 hours ♥ yields: 4 parfaits

At my first blog conference in Miami, the host hotel's kitchen set out a colorful array of appetizers and desserts after a full day of presentations. With a rumbling stomach, I immediately reached for one of the sweet treats: a miniature layered parfait topped with a large white chocolate curl. It left quite an impression—I finished the first glass in the blink of an eye and quickly reached for a second! Those parfaits served as the inspiration for this recipe, especially the white chocolate garnish on top.

- 1 cup (240g) plain nonfat Greek yogurt
- 1 serving (7g) fat-free, sugar-free lemon instant pudding mix
- 7 tbsp (11g) granulated sucralose
- 1 cup (140g) fresh raspberries
- 1 tbsp (14g) white chocolate chips, finely chopped

1. Beat the Greek yogurt, instant pudding mix, and granulated sucralose in a medium bowl on low speed for 2 minutes or until thickened. Chill for at least 2 hours.
2. To assemble, alternate between adding the prepared lemon pudding and fresh raspberries to 4 small parfait glasses. Top with a sprinkle of white chocolate.

AMY'S ADVICE
If chilling the pudding longer than 2 hours, cover the top of the bowl with foil or transfer the pudding to a container with a tight-fitting lid.

GF   HP

Nutrition Information: 62 calories | 0.6g fat (0.3g saturated fat, 0.1g unsaturated fat) | 0.2mg cholesterol 102.3mg sodium | 7.4g carbohydrates (2.1g fiber, 2.3g sugar) | 6.1g protein

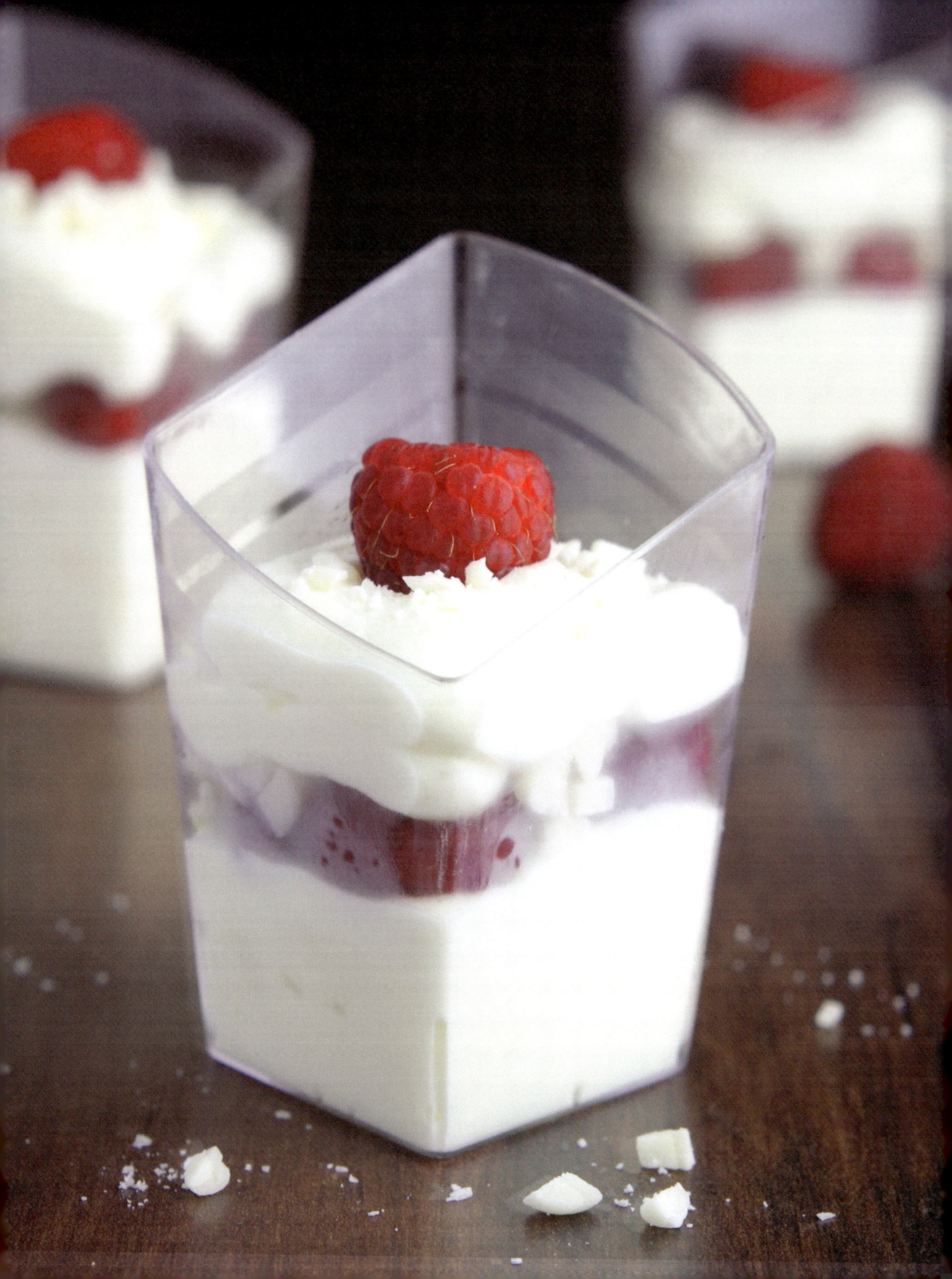

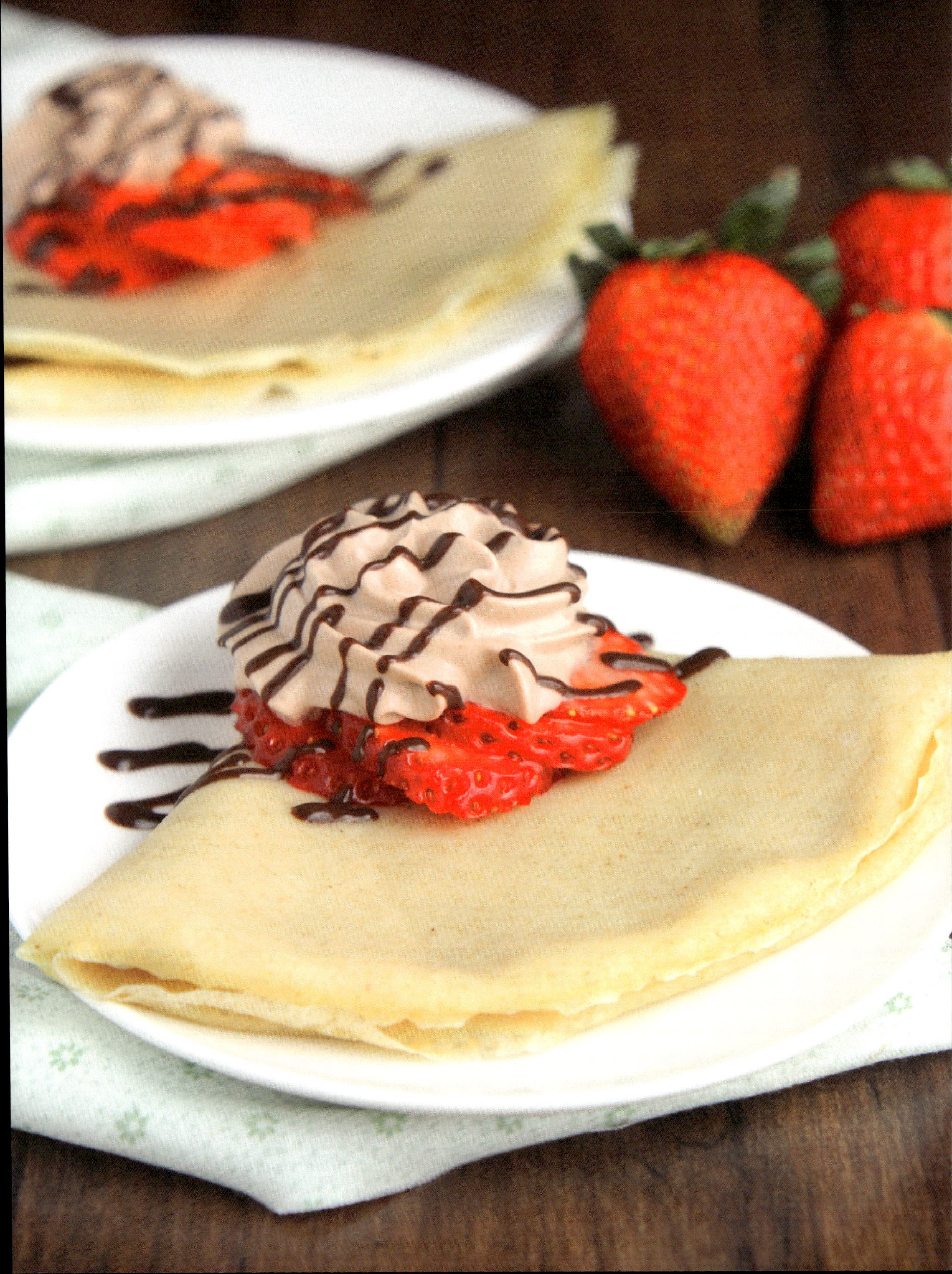

STRAWBERRY & CHOCOLATE WHIPPED CREAM CRÊPES

prep time: 20 minutes ♥ inactive time: 10 minutes
cooking time: 30 minutes ♥ yields: 8 crêpes

In high school, my brother learned how to make authentic crêpes from his best friend's French mother. He offered to cook them nearly every time we hosted a weekend brunch, and eventually I asked him to teach me the techniques. While these healthier crêpes aren't quite as traditional as the French lady's recipe, they still taste just as delicious—especially with the chocolate whipped cream!

for topping
- 3 tbsp (45mL) heavy cream
- 2 tbsp (24g) Confectioners Style Swerve®
- 6 tbsp (90g) plain nonfat Greek yogurt
- 1 tsp vanilla extract
- 1 tbsp (5g) unsweetened cocoa powder
- 8 large strawberries, thinly sliced

for the crêpes
- 1 large egg, room temperature
- 1 large egg white, room temperature
- 1 cup (240mL) nonfat milk, room temperature
- 1 tsp agave
- 1 tsp vanilla extract
- ⅞ cup (105g) whole wheat pastry flour, sifted

1. To prepare the chocolate whipped cream, place the metal beater attachment(s) and a medium glass or metal bowl into the freezer for 5 minutes. Once cold, remove the beater(s) and bowl. Add the heavy cream to the bowl, and beat until it reaches the soft peak stage, or until it has thickened and doubled in size. Add the remaining ingredients, and beat until the mixture reaches the stiff peak stage. Chill the whipped cream until ready to serve.

2. To prepare the crêpes, whisk together the egg, egg white, milk, agave, and vanilla in a large bowl until frothy. Gradually whisk in the flour until fully incorporated. Let the batter rest for 10 minutes.

3. Preheat a large 8" pan over low heat, and lightly coat with nonstick cooking spray. When the pan is warm, scoop ¼ cup of batter using a ⅓-measuring cup, quickly add it to the center of the pan, and pick up the pan to swirl around the batter to completely cover the bottom. Place the pan back down on the burner. Let the crêpe sit until the batter looks fully cooked. Loosen the edges using a spatula, and remove onto a plate. Re-coat the pan with cooking spray, and repeat with the remaining batter, placing a paper towel in between each crêpe to avoid sticking.

4. To assemble, fold each crêpe into quarters. Top with 1 strawberry's slices and a dollop of chocolate whipped cream.

Nutrition Information: 108 calories | 3.3g fat (1.5g saturated fat, 1.1g unsaturated fat) 31.6mg cholesterol | 44.1mg sodium 14.7g carbohydrates (2.4g fiber, 3.8g sugar) 5.5g protein

CHOCOLATE PUDDING PIE

prep time: 15 minutes ♥ baking time: 10 minutes
inactive time: 2 hours ♥ yields: 8 slices

During my senior year, I played the flute in the orchestra for our high school's musical. After our evening performance on "Pi Day," March 14, a few of us drove to a diner across town for celebratory slices of pie. As a chocoholic, I ordered the most chocolaty slice on the menu, and this recipe is a healthier—and much easier—version of it.

12 full sheets (186g) chocolate graham crackers
1 tbsp (14g) unsalted butter, melted
2 large egg whites, room temperature
1 (2.1oz) package fat-free, sugar-free chocolate instant pudding mix
2 ½ cups (600mL) nonfat milk

1. Preheat the oven to 350°F, and lightly coat a 9" pie plate with nonstick cooking spray.
2. Add the graham crackers to a food processor or blender, and pulse until they're fine crumbs. Add the crumbs to a bowl, and mix in the butter and egg whites. Press the mixture into the bottom and up the sides of the pie plate. Bake at 350°F for 10 minutes. Cool completely.
3. Once the pie crust has cooled, add the pudding mix and milk to a large bowl. Beat on low speed for 2 minutes. Immediately spread the pudding into the prepared pie crust, and chill for at least 2 hours before serving.

AMY'S ADVICE
Try other pudding mix flavors like vanilla or cheesecake for a fun twist!

Nutrition Information: 164 calories | 3.8g fat (1.7g saturated fat, 1.6g unsaturated fat) | 5.4mg cholesterol 398.3mg sodium | 27.3g carbohydrates (1.4g fiber, 10.7g sugar) | 5.7g protein

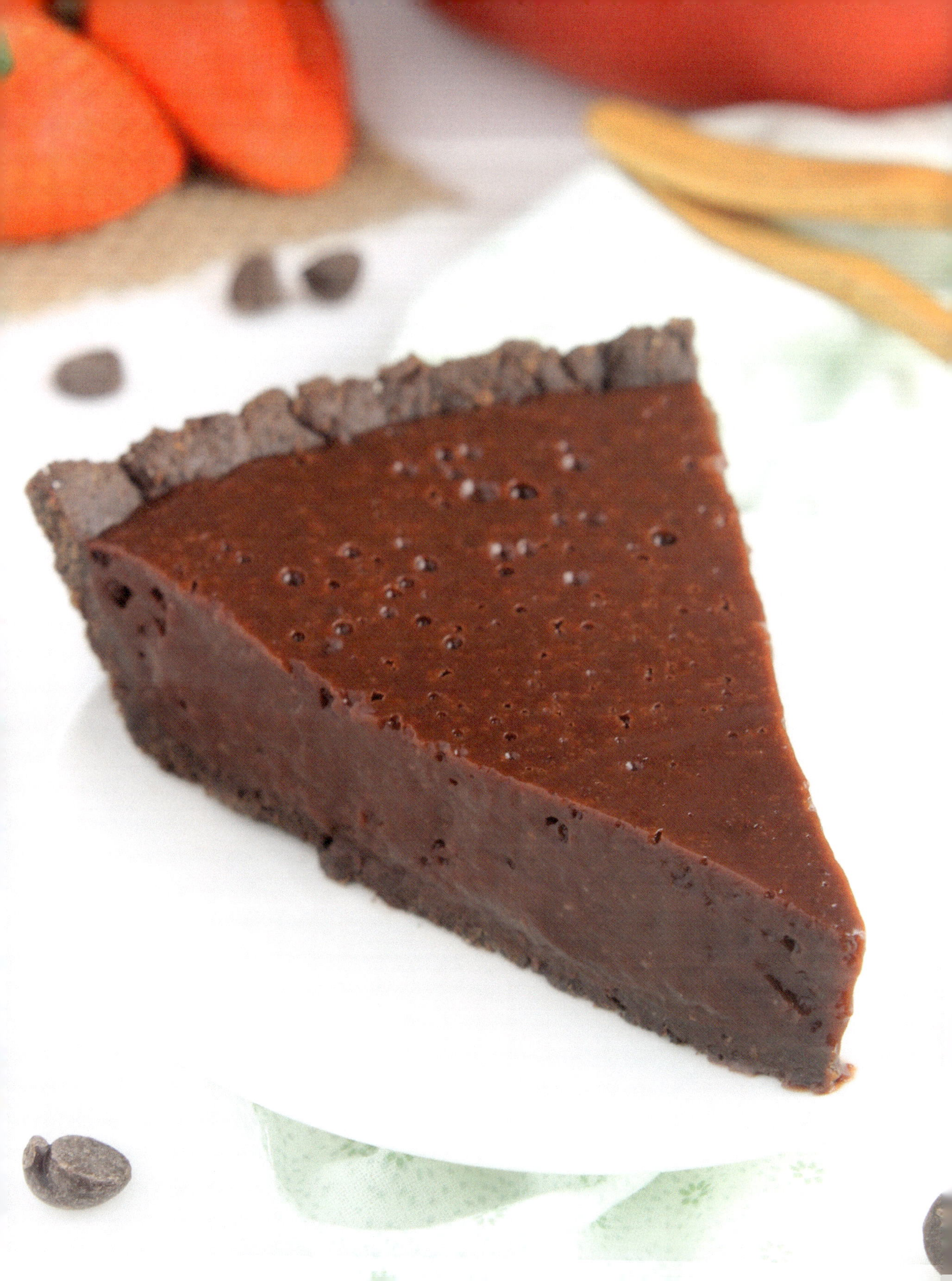

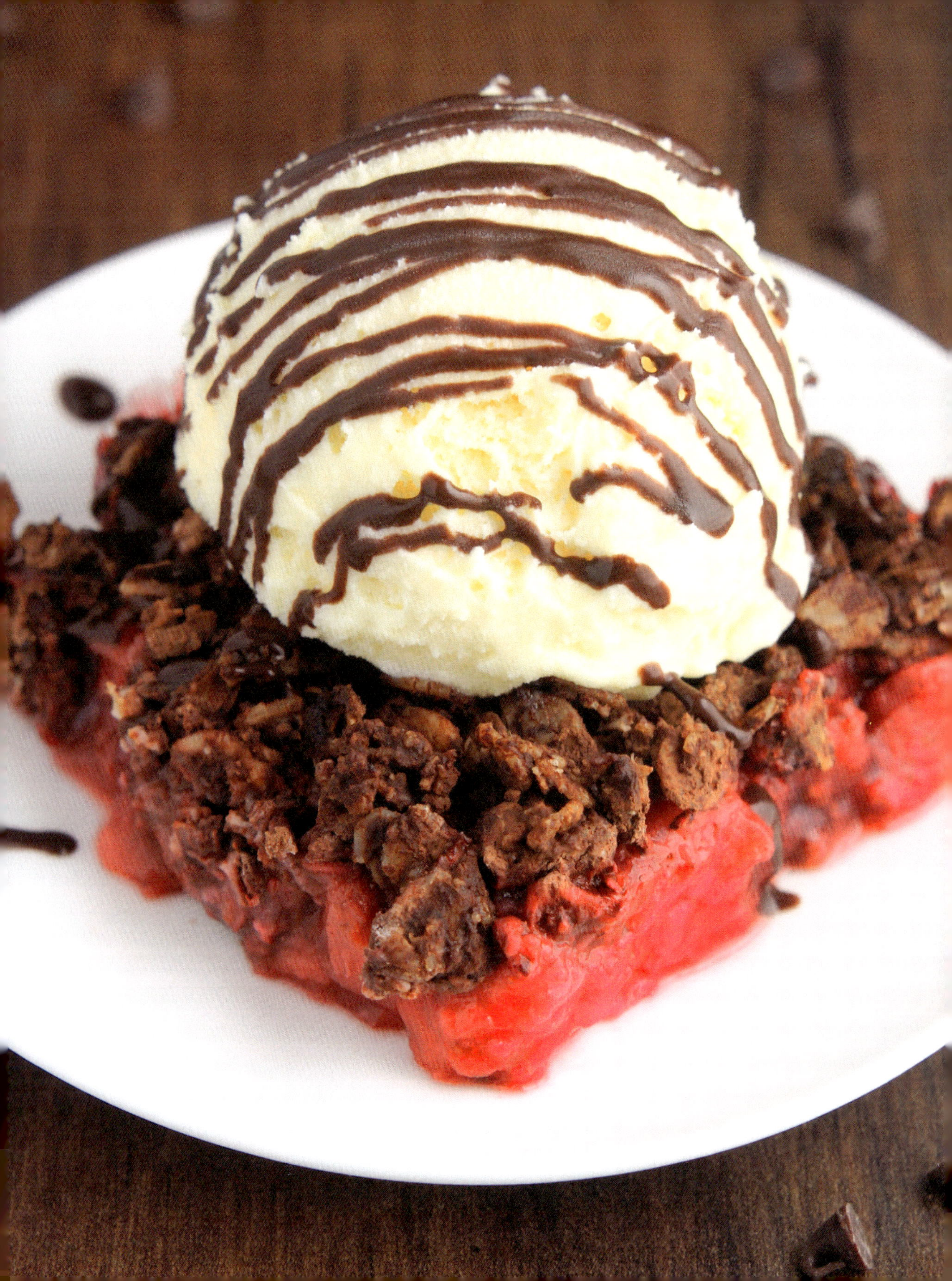

DARK CHOCOLATE STRAWBERRY CRUMBLE

prep time: 25 minutes ♥ baking time: 55-65 minutes
inactive time: 4 hours ♥ yields: 9 servings

For spring break during my first year of college, my dad and I flew to Arizona to visit my aunt and go to a few Major League Baseball spring training games. Since my aunt knew I preferred healthy food, she cooked lighter stuffed bell peppers for dinner on our first night and a fruit crumble for dessert. The next morning while my aunt and dad sat at the table sipping their mugs of coffee, I quietly opened the refrigerator to sneak a few more bites of the fruity dessert! Although she passed away a few years later, baking crumbles still reminds me of our visit and those nights where we enjoyed many servings of my aunt's fruit dessert.

¾ cup (75g) old-fashioned oats
¼ cup (20g) unsweetened cocoa powder
1 tsp ground cinnamon
2 tbsp (28g) unsalted butter, melted
2 tbsp (30mL) agave
6 cups (840g) frozen unsweetened strawberries, thawed slightly and chopped
3 tbsp (24g) cornstarch
reduced fat vanilla ice cream, for serving (optional)

1. Preheat the oven to 350°F, and lightly coat an 8"-square pan with nonstick cooking spray.
2. To prepare the crumb topping, combine the oats, cocoa powder, and cinnamon in a small bowl. Stir in the butter and agave until all of the dry ingredients are fully incorporated. To prepare the filling, toss together the strawberries and cornstarch in a large bowl until the strawberries are evenly coated.
3. Evenly spread the filling into the prepared pan, and sprinkle with the crumb topping. Bake at 350°F for 55-65 minutes or until the fruit juices are bubbling. Cool the crumble completely to room temperature. Cover the pan with foil, and chill for at least 3 hours before serving with vanilla ice cream.

Nutrition Information: 111 calories | 3.4g fat (1.6g saturated fat, 1.2g unsaturated fat) | 6.9mg cholesterol
31.3mg sodium | 21.0g carbohydrates (3.8g fiber, 8.3g sugar) | 1.8g protein

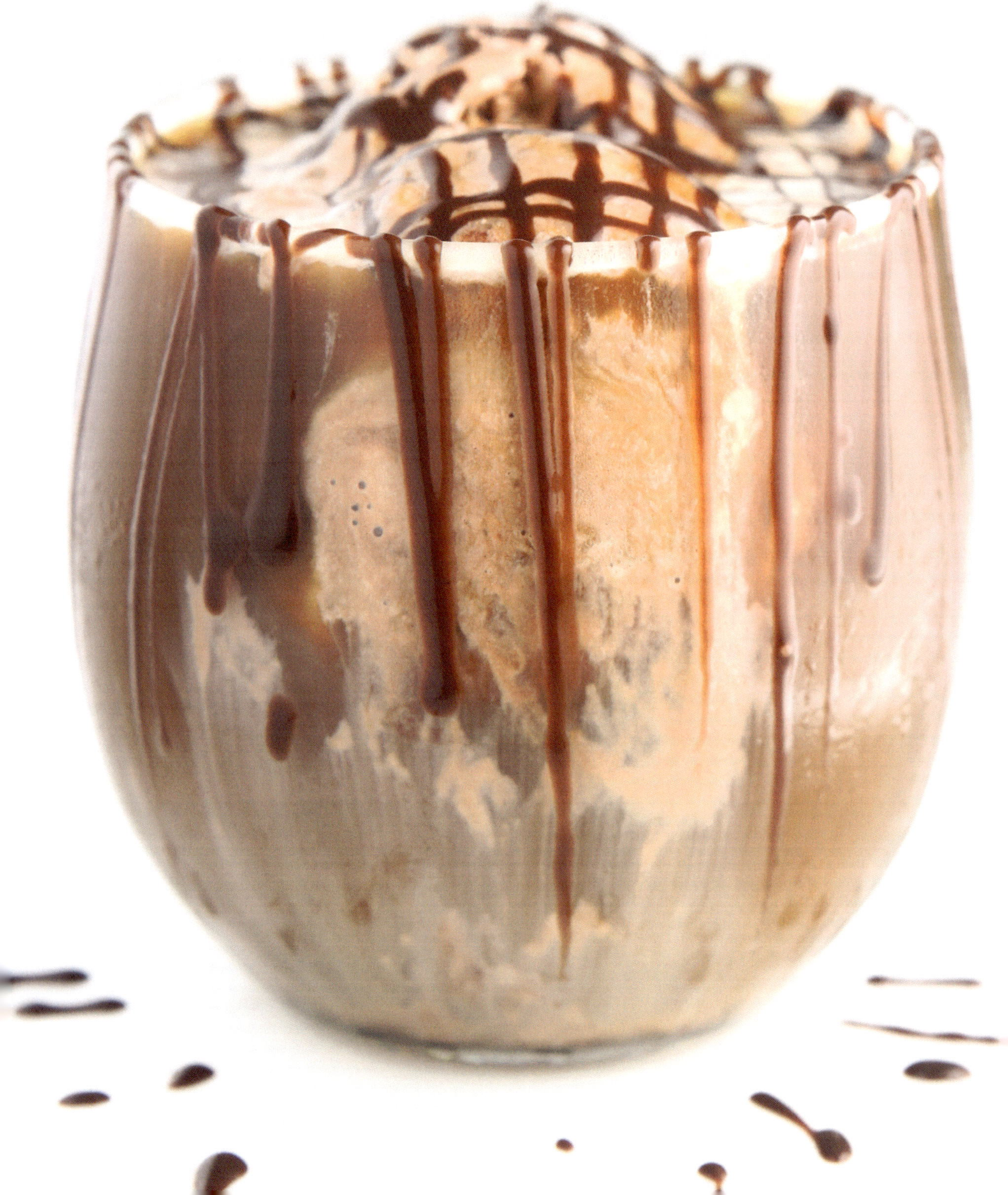

MOCHA ICE CREAM FLOAT

prep time: 3 minutes ♥ yields: 1 float

Every once in a while, my guy and I visit a dessert diner located in the heart of downtown. Since he isn't a big dessert fan, he usually orders an ice cream soda float while I select a slice of cake. On one particularly busy Friday night when the line snaked through the restaurant, I scanned the menu boards while we waited and spotted an espresso float right next to the soda options. Because I refused to give up my favorite slice of fancy cake, I decided to try making my own coffee version at home instead—with the most chocolaty ice cream I could find, of course!

- ½ cup (62g) reduced fat triple chocolate ice cream
- 1 cup (240mL) strong brewed coffee, chilled

1. Add the ice cream to a medium glass, and slowly pour the coffee on top.

GF

Nutrition Information: 115 calories | 3.5g fat (2.0g saturated fat, 0.0g unsaturated fat) | 10.0mg cholesterol 75.0mg sodium | 17.0g carbohydrates (2.0g fiber, 3.0g sugar) | 3.0g protein

SUGAR COOKIE CHOCOLATE ICE CREAM SANDWICHES

prep time: 35 minutes ♥ baking time: 8-11 minutes
inactive time: 2 hours ♥ yields: 15 sandwiches

Nearly every summer during our childhood, my brother and I would ask our mom if we could buy ice cream sandwiches during the adult swim time at the community pool. Every so often she agreed, and we usually found a few drops of melty ice cream dribbling down our fingers from savoring them too slowly. For these homemade ice cream sandwiches, I turned the flavors inside out—the cookies are now vanilla and the ice cream (the best part) contains triple the chocolate!

- 1 ¼ cups (150g) all-purpose flour
- ¾ tsp cornstarch
- ¼ tsp baking powder
- ¼ tsp salt
- 2 tbsp (28g) unsalted butter, melted and cooled slightly
- 1 large egg, room temperature
- 1 tsp vanilla extract
- ½ tsp butter extract
- ⅝ cup (132g) granulated sugar
- 2 ⅞ cups (357g) reduced fat triple chocolate ice cream

1. Whisk together the flour, cornstarch, baking powder, and salt in a medium bowl. In a separate bowl, whisk together the butter, egg, vanilla, and butter extract. Stir in the granulated sugar. Add the flour mixture, stirring until just incorporated.
2. Transfer the cookie dough onto a large piece of plastic wrap. Shape the cookie dough into a 1"-thick rectangle using a spatula. Seal the cookie dough inside of the plastic wrap, and chill for 1 hour.
3. Preheat the oven to 350°F, and line two baking sheets with silicone baking mats or parchment paper.
4. On a well-floured surface, roll out the cookie dough to ⅛" thick. Cut out rounds using 2 ½" wide circular cookie cutters. Transfer the cutouts to the prepared baking sheets. Reroll any extra cookie dough, and cut out additional rounds.
5. Bake at 350°F for 8-11 minutes. Cool on the pan for 5 minutes before transferring to a wire rack to cool completely.
6. To assemble the ice cream sandwiches, place 3 tablespoons of ice cream on top of one sugar cookie, and top with a second cookie. Gently press down, and freeze the sandwiches on a baking tray until ready to serve.

Nutrition Information: 134 calories | 3.3g fat (1.8g saturated fat, 0.8g unsaturated fat) | 20.4mg cholesterol
77.0mg sodium | 23.5g carbohydrates (1.0g fiber, 10.0g sugar) | 2.7g protein

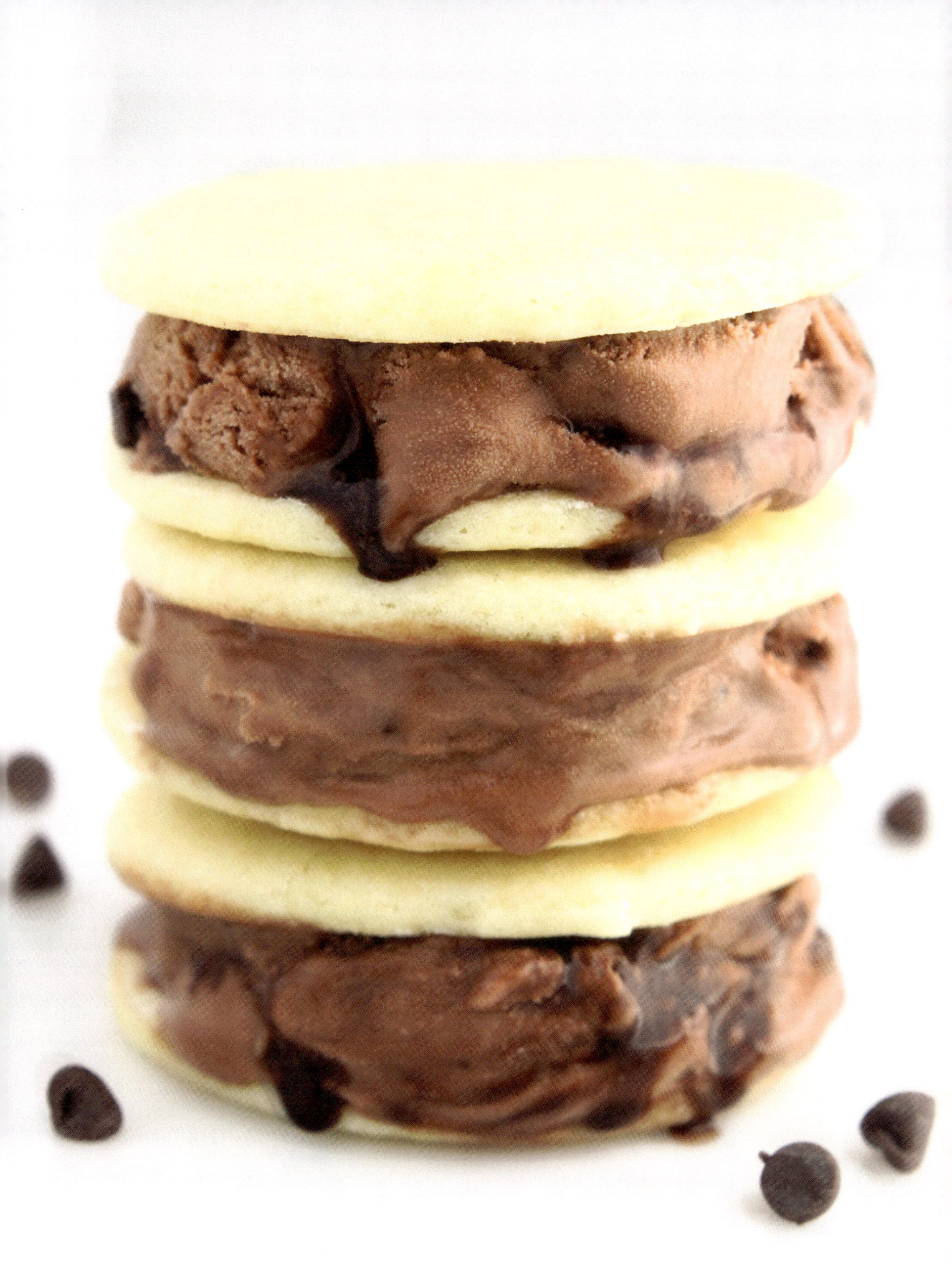

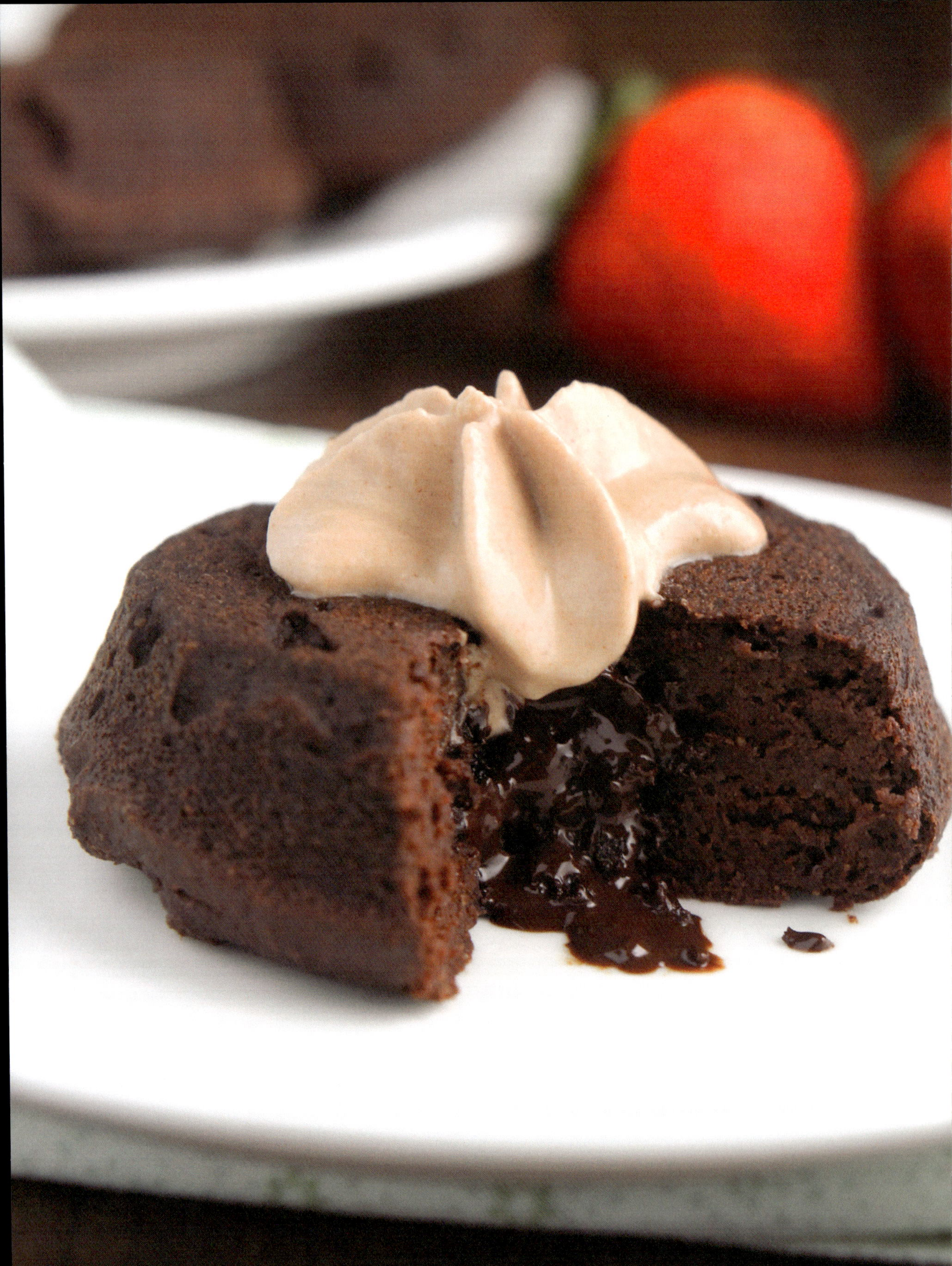

MINI DARK CHOCOLATE LAVA CAKES

prep time: 15 minutes ♥ baking time: 18 minutes ♥ yields: 4 cakes

In high school, my close friend and I cooked a gourmet dinner for her family, complete with decadent chocolate lava cakes. My mom arrived to pick me up just as we started serving dessert, so she sat down at the table with us to enjoy the rich gooey centers warm from the oven. In this easier version, I pressed a small piece of dark chocolate into the batter before baking to ensure the centers are as decadent and melty as possible.

- ⅓ cup (27g) unsweetened cocoa powder
- ¼ cup (30g) white whole wheat flour
- ¼ tsp baking powder
- ⅛ tsp salt
- ½ tbsp (7g) unsalted butter, melted and cooled slightly
- 1 large egg white, room temperature
- ¾ tsp vanilla extract
- 2 tbsp (30g) plain nonfat Greek yogurt
- 2 tbsp (30mL) maple syrup
- 2 tbsp (30mL) nonfat milk
- 4 small (4g each) squares dark chocolate

1. Preheat the oven to 325°F, and lightly coat 4 muffin cups with nonstick cooking spray.
2. Whisk together the cocoa powder, flour, baking powder, and salt in a small bowl. In a separate bowl, whisk together the butter, egg white, and vanilla. Stir in the Greek yogurt, mixing until no large lumps remain. Mix in the maple syrup. Alternate between adding the flour mixture and milk to the egg white mixture, beginning and ending with the flour mixture, and stirring until just incorporated.
3. Divide the batter between the prepared muffin cups, and gently press 1 dark chocolate square into the center of each. Use a spatula to spread the batter over the top of the dark chocolate, if necessary. Bake at 325°F for 18 minutes or until the top feels lightly firm to the touch. Cool the lava cakes in the muffin cups for 5 minutes before inverting and serving.

AMY'S ADVICE

I recommend Trader Joe's® small bars of 72% dark chocolate! They're sold up near the registers in red wrappers in 3-packs. To reheat, microwave individual lava cakes for 10-13 seconds.

Nutrition Information: 115 calories | 3.9g fat (1.9g saturated fat, 0.5g unsaturated fat) | 4.0mg cholesterol 214.6mg sodium | 19.1g carbohydrates (4.1g fiber, 7.9g sugar) | 4.6g protein

CHOCOLATE STRAWBERRY SHORTCAKES

prep time: 20 minutes ♥ baking time: 13-15 minutes
inactive time: 45 minutes ♥ yields: 9 shortcakes

During high school, two of my friends asked for Baking Lessons after I walked into their kitchen to find them struggling to follow the directions on the back of a package of cookie dough mix. They requested strawberry shortcake as one of the first recipes, and we were all surprised by how easy the shortcakes were to bake. While we topped that first set with store-bought whipped cream, these healthier ones of mine uses a homemade chocolate recipe that makes them even better than the traditional version.

for the shortcakes
1 ½ cups (180g) whole wheat pastry flour
1 tsp baking powder
½ tsp baking soda
¼ tsp salt
3 tbsp (42g) unsalted butter, cold and cubed
½ cup (120g) plain nonfat Greek yogurt
2 tbsp (30mL) nonfat milk
1 tbsp (15mL) vanilla extract
1 ¼ cups (175g) fresh strawberries, thinly sliced

for the whipped cream
3 tbsp (45mL) heavy cream
2 tbsp (24g) Confectioners Style Swerve®
6 tbsp (90g) plain nonfat Greek yogurt
1 tsp vanilla extract
1 tbsp (5g) unsweetened cocoa powder

C

Nutrition Information: 152 calories | 6.5g fat (3.5g saturated fat, 1.9g unsaturated fat) 17.3mg cholesterol | 210.3mg sodium 18.6g carbohydrates (3.3g fiber, 2.3g sugar) 5.4g protein

1. Preheat the oven to 425°F, and lightly coat an 8"-square pan with nonstick cooking spray.
2. To prepare the shortcakes, whisk together the flour, baking powder, baking soda, and salt in a large bowl. Cut in the cold butter using a pastry cutter or the back of a fork until the mixture resembles fine crumbs. Stir in the Greek yogurt, milk, and vanilla.
3. Gently press the dough into the prepared pan. Bake at 425°F for 13-15 minutes or until the edges begin to turn light golden and the center feels lightly firm. Cool in the pan for 10 minutes before inverting and transferring to a wire rack to cool completely.
4. While the shortcakes bake, prepare the chocolate whipped cream. Place the metal beater attachment(s) and a medium glass or metal bowl into the freezer for 5 minutes. Once cold, remove the beater(s) and bowl. Add the heavy cream to the bowl, and beat until it reaches the soft peak stage, or until it has thickened and doubled in size. Add the remaining ingredients, and beat until the mixture reaches the stiff peak stage. Chill the whipped cream until ready to serve.
5. To assemble, slice the shortcake into 9 squares, and carefully slice each square in half horizontally. Layer the sliced strawberries on the bottom shortcake half, pipe a dollop of whipped cream on top, and finish with the top shortcake half.

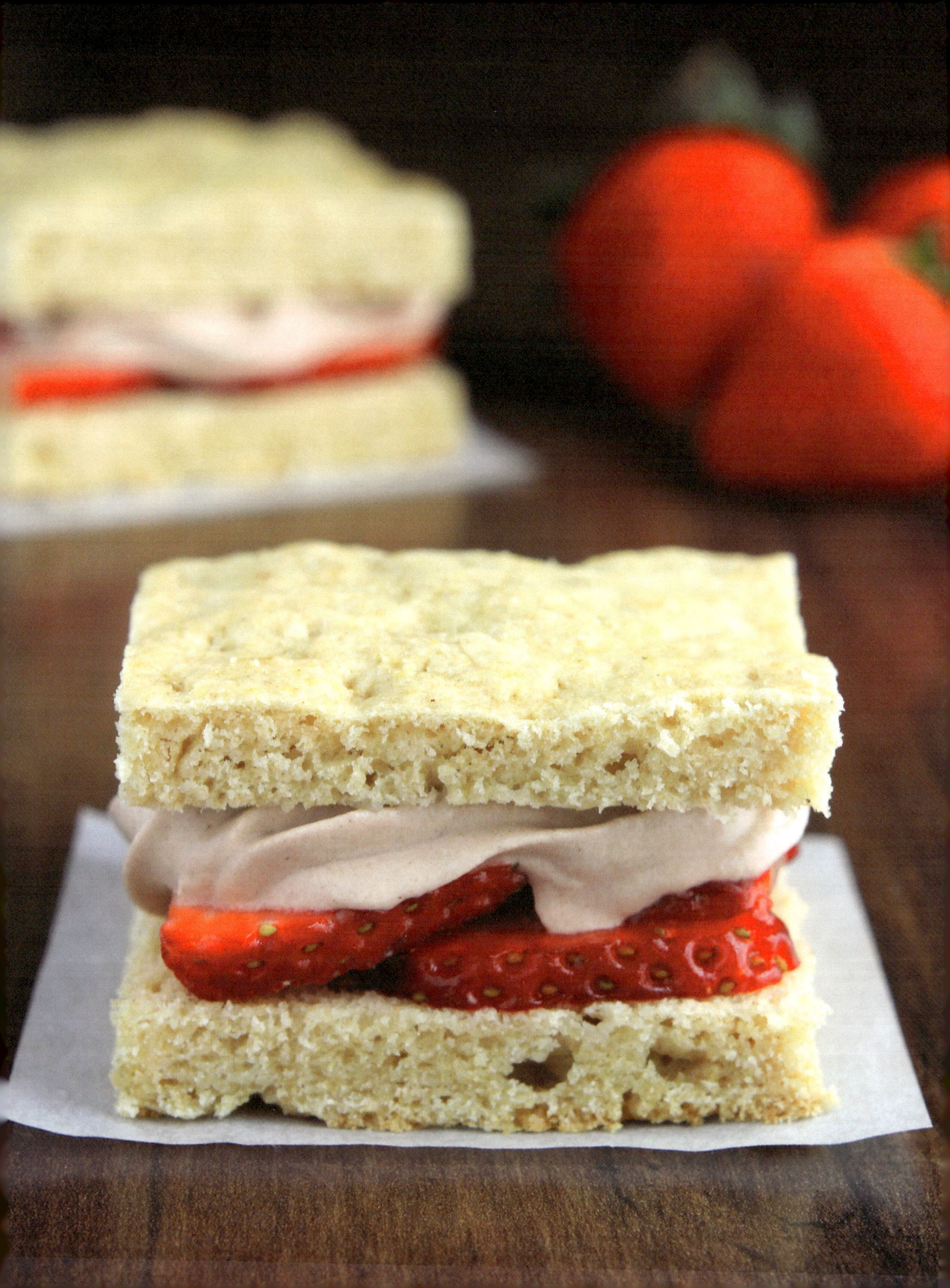

DARK CHOCOLATE CUPCAKES

prep time: 20 minutes ♥ baking time: 21 minutes
inactive time: 2 hours ♥ yields: 12 cupcakes

Before I began blogging full-time, I barely had any time or energy during the week to bake because of the long hours spent at my chemistry job, so on the nights where I desperately craved a chocolate dessert, I stopped by the gourmet grocery store on my way home from work to stare at the display case in their fancy bakery department. After sampling a few of the treats, I picked their decadent double chocolate cupcakes as my favorite—not surprising for a chocoholic like me! These are my healthier version, they taste even more chocolaty than those store-bought ones.

for the cupcakes
- 1 cup (80g) unsweetened cocoa powder
- ¾ cup (90g) all-purpose flour
- 2 tsp baking powder
- ¼ tsp salt
- 2 tbsp (28g) unsalted butter, melted and cooled slightly
- 2 large eggs, room temperature
- 1 tbsp (15mL) vanilla extract
- ⅔ cup (128g) granulated sugar
- ¼ cup (60g) plain nonfat Greek yogurt
- ½ cup (120mL) nonfat milk

for the frosting
- 2 cups (480g) plain nonfat Greek yogurt
- 2 servings (14g) sugar-free, fat-free chocolate instant pudding mix
- ½ cup (12g) granulated sucralose
- ¼ cup (20g) unsweetened cocoa powder

1. Preheat the oven to 350°F. Line 12 muffin cups with cupcake liners, and generously coat with nonstick cooking spray.
2. To prepare the cupcakes, whisk together the cocoa powder, flour, baking powder, and salt in a medium bowl. In a separate bowl, whisk together the butter, eggs, and vanilla. Stir in the sugar. Mix in the Greek yogurt, stirring until no large lumps remain. Alternate between adding the flour mixture and milk, beginning and ending with the flour mixture, and stirring until just incorporated. (For best results, add the flour mixture in 3 equal parts.)
3. Divide the batter between the prepared muffin cups. Bake at 350°F for 21 minutes or until the tops feel firm to the touch. Cool the cupcakes in the muffin cups for 5 minutes before transferring them to a wire rack to cool completely.
4. While the cupcakes bake, prepare the frosting. Beat the Greek yogurt instant pudding mix, sucralose, and cocoa powder in a large bowl for 2 minutes or until thickened. Chill for 2 hours before piping on top of the cooled cupcakes.

Nutrition Information: 147 calories | 3.6g fat (1.5g saturated fat, 1.2g unsaturated fat) | 36.4mg cholesterol 303.3mg sodium | 25.1g carbohydrates (3.5g fiber, 13.1g sugar) | 7.3g protein

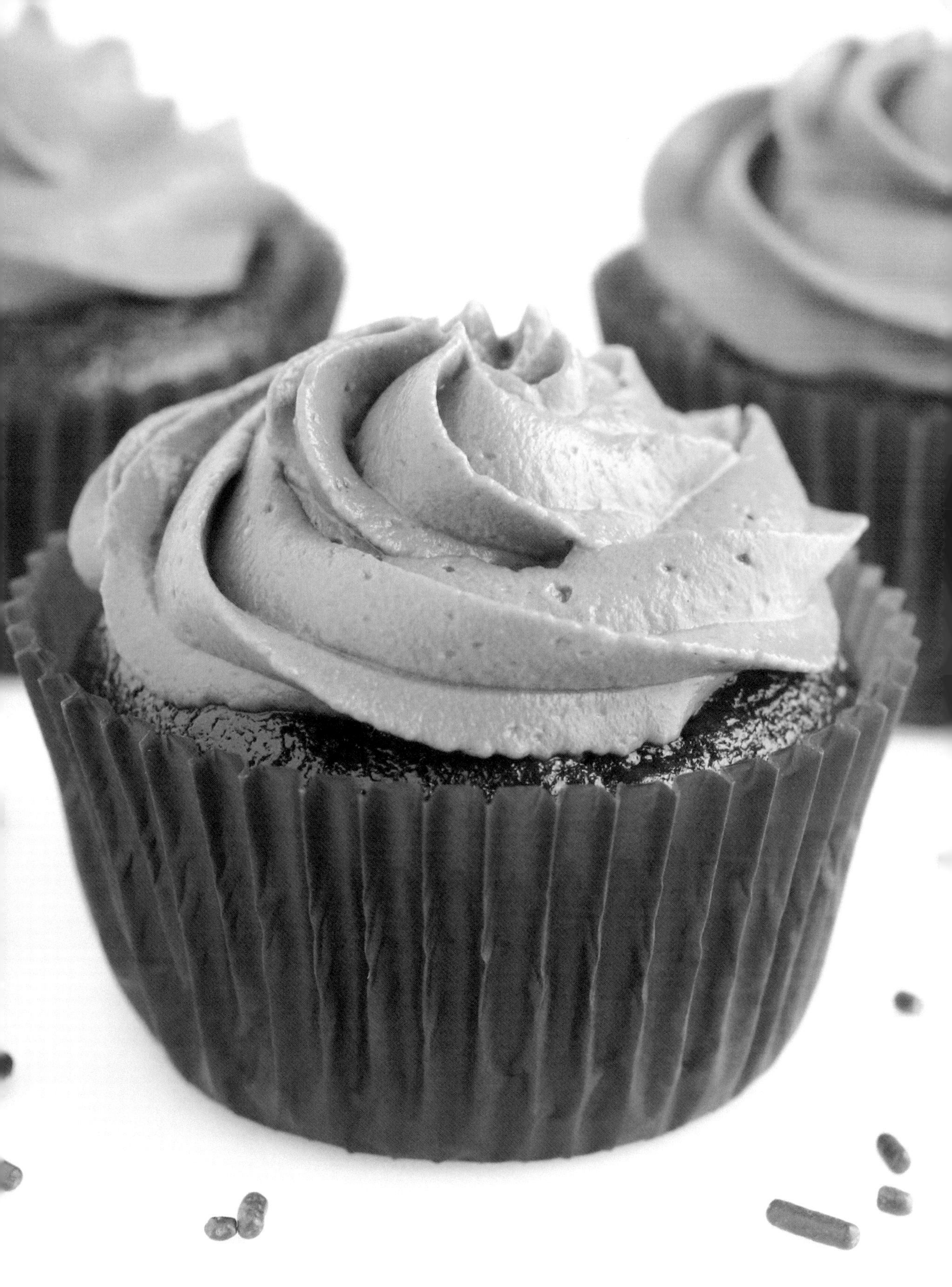

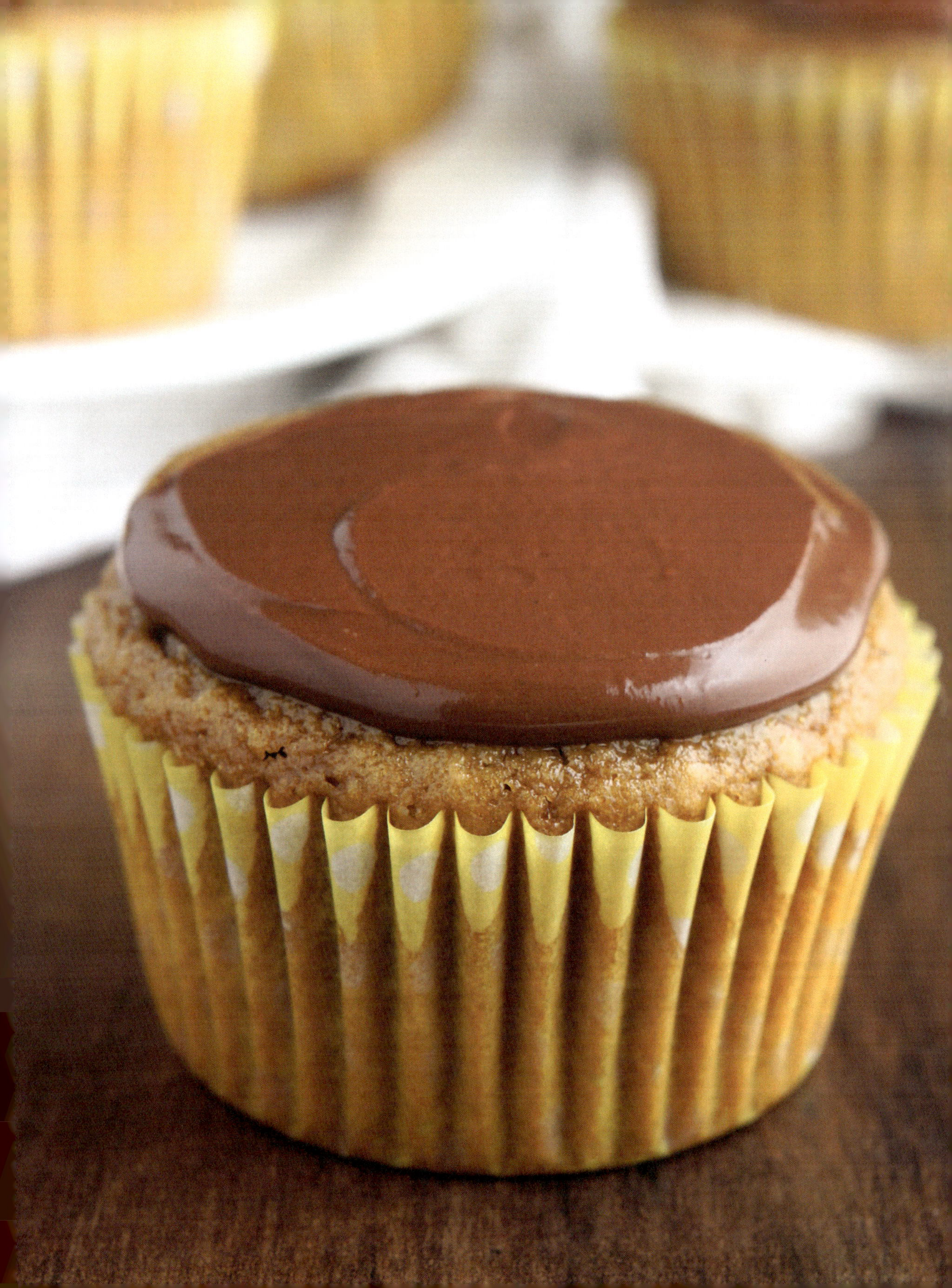

DARK CHOCOLATE FROSTED VANILLA CUPCAKES

prep time: 25 minutes ♥ baking time: 22 minutes
inactive time: 1 hour ♥ yields: 12 cupcakes

In high school, my friends and I threw a Halloween party in August, complete with costumes, semi-scary cartoon movies, and bobbing for apples. For dessert, one friend and I baked vanilla cupcakes, and I meticulously spread dark chocolate frosting on top of each one, swirling the knife all the way to the edges of the wrapper to add as much frosting as possible, before showering them with festive Halloween sprinkles. Although we used a box mix and canned frosting back then, these healthier cupcakes are made entirely from scratch, and I had an even harder time keeping my finger out of the frosting bowl!

for the cupcakes
1 ¾ cups (210g) whole wheat pastry flour
¾ tsp baking powder
¾ tsp baking soda
½ tsp salt
1 tbsp (14g) unsalted butter, melted and cooled slightly
2 large eggs, room temperature
1 tbsp (15mL) vanilla extract
¼ cup (60g) plain nonfat Greek yogurt
¾ cup (180mL) agave
¼ cup (60mL) nonfat milk

for the frosting
½ cup (40g) unsweetened cocoa powder
¼ cup (60g) plain nonfat Greek yogurt
2 tbsp (30mL) agave
¼ cup (60mL) nonfat milk

1. Preheat the oven to 325°F. Line 12 muffin cups with cupcake liners, and generously coat with nonstick cooking spray.

2. To prepare the cupcakes, whisk together the flour, baking powder, baking soda, and salt in a medium bowl. In a separate bowl, whisk together the butter, eggs, and vanilla. Stir in the Greek yogurt, mixing until no large lumps remain. Stir in the agave. Alternate between adding the flour mixture and the milk, beginning and ending with the flour, and stirring until just incorporated. (For best results, add the flour mixture in 3 equal parts.)

3. Divide the batter between the prepared muffin cups. Bake at 325°F for 22 minutes or until the tops feel firm to the touch. Cool the cupcakes in the muffin cups for 5 minutes before transferring to a wire rack to cool completely.

4. To prepare the frosting, stir together the cocoa powder, Greek yogurt, agave, and milk in a medium bowl until smooth. Spread on top of the cooled cupcakes.

Nutrition Information: 172 calories | 2.7g fat (0.9g saturated fat, 0.8g unsaturated fat) | 33.8mg cholesterol 270.1mg sodium | 35.3g carbohydrates (3.7g fiber, 19.7g sugar) | 5.4g protein

COCONUT CAKE WITH DARK CHOCOLATE FROSTING

prep time: 35 minutes ♥ baking time: 18-20 minutes
inactive time: 2 hours ♥ yields: 12 servings

Besides double lemon, German chocolate is my dad's favorite cake flavor, and I usually bake one of the two for his birthday every fall. Instead of sticking with the traditional version one year, I turned the flavors inside out and made a coconut cake with chocolate frosting. It was a huge hit, especially that fudgy frosting… We ate the extra with spoons straight from the bowl!

for the cake
1 ¾ cups (210g) whole wheat pastry flour
1 ½ tsp baking powder
½ tsp baking soda
¼ tsp salt
1 tbsp (14g) coconut oil, melted
1 large egg, room temperature
2 tsp coconut extract
1 tsp vanilla extract
½ cup (120g) plain nonfat Greek yogurt
1 cup (192g) coconut sugar
½ cup (120mL) nonfat milk

for the frosting
¼ cup (56g) chopped dark chocolate
2 tbsp (30mL) warm nonfat milk
¾ cup (180g) plain nonfat Greek yogurt, room temperature
5 tbsp (25g) unsweetened cocoa powder
1 tbsp (13g) Truvia®

1. Preheat the oven to 350°F. Line two 9"-round baking pans with wax paper, and lightly coat with nonstick cooking spray.

2. To prepare the cake, whisk together the flour, baking powder, baking soda, and salt in a medium bowl. In a separate bowl, whisk together the coconut oil, egg, coconut extract, and vanilla extract. Stir in the Greek yogurt, mixing until no large lumps remain. Stir in the coconut sugar. Alternate between adding the flour mixture and milk, beginning and ending with the flour mixture, and stirring until just incorporated. (For best results, add the flour mixture in 3 equal parts.)

3. Spread the batter into the prepared pans. Bake at 350°F for 18-20 minutes or until a toothpick inserted into the center comes out clean. Cool the cake layers in the pans for 10 minutes before inverting, peeling off the wax paper, and transferring to wire racks. Cool the cake layers completely to room temperature.

4. To prepare the frosting, add the chopped dark chocolate to a microwave-safe bowl. Microwave the bowl on HIGH for 20 seconds. Stir, and microwave on HIGH for another 10 seconds. Stir until smooth. Add the warm milk, stirring until incorporated. Mix in the Greek yogurt, cocoa powder, and Truvia® until smooth.

5. To assemble the cake, spread frosting on top of one layer. Place the other layer on top. Spread frosting on top of the second layer and around the sides of the cake.

Nutrition Information: 195 calories | 4.7g fat (2.1g saturated fat, 0.3g unsaturated fat)
30.9mg cholesterol | 275.6mg sodium
32.8g carbohydrates (3.3g fiber, 17.7g sugar)
7.8g protein

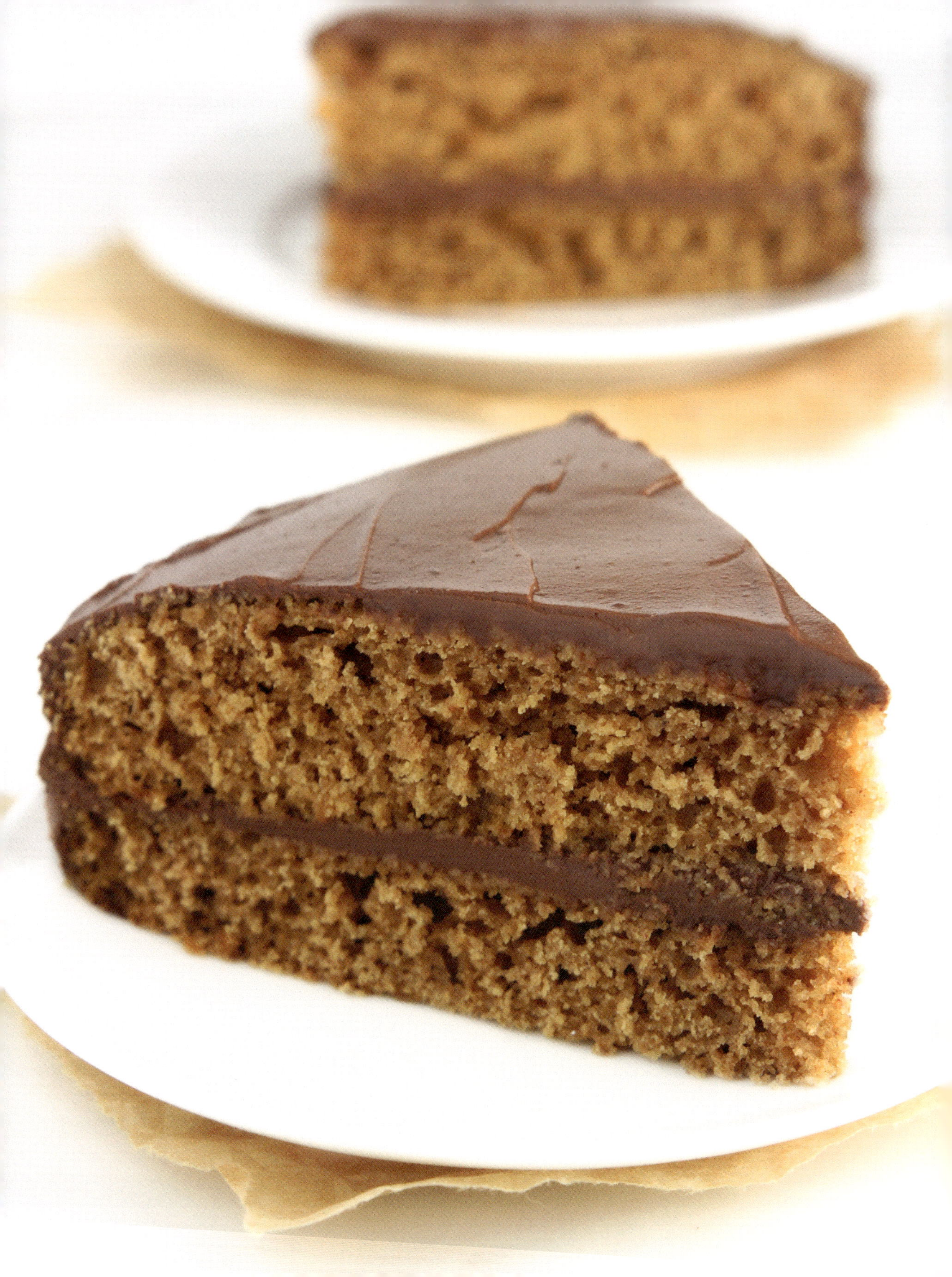

DARK CHOCOLATE DRIZZLED COFFEE BUNDT CAKE

prep time: 20 minutes ♥ baking time: 40-45 minutes
inactive time: 2 hours ♥ yields: 14 servings

Throughout my childhood, my parents and grandparents loved dining at a particular brunch restaurant famous for their cinnamon-spiced hot tea and crumb-topped coffee cake. Since I had accidentally tried a sip of my dad's strong black coffee at a very young age, I could never understand why anyone would want to eat cake with that bitter flavor, especially for breakfast! Eventually I learned that "coffee cake" earned its name because it was meant to be enjoyed alongside coffee... But more than 15 years later when I gave coffee another try and fell in love, I decided to bake the other type of "coffee cake" with the flavors I imagined as a child.

for the cake
¾ cup (180mL) warm nonfat milk (90-100°F)
3 tbsp (6g) instant coffee crystals
3 cups (360g) white whole wheat flour
1 ½ tsp baking powder
¾ tsp baking soda
½ tsp salt
2 tbsp (28g) unsalted butter, melted and cooled slightly
1 large egg, room temperature
1 large egg white, room temperature
1 tbsp (15mL) vanilla extract
¾ cup (180g) plain nonfat Greek yogurt
¾ cup (180mL) maple syrup

for the drizzle
3 tbsp (15g) unsweetened cocoa powder
1 ½ tsp agave
2 tbsp (30mL) nonfat milk

1. Preheat the oven to 350°F, and generously coat a 12-cup bundt pan with nonstick baking spray with flour.
2. To prepare the cake, add the warm milk and instant coffee to a small bowl. Stir to combine, and set the bowl aside to allow the coffee to dissolve.
3. Whisk together the flour, baking powder, baking soda, and salt in a medium bowl. In a separate bowl, whisk together the butter, egg, egg white, and vanilla. Stir in the Greek yogurt, mixing until no large lumps remain. Stir in the maple syrup. Alternate between adding the flour mixture and milk mixture, beginning and ending with the flour, and stirring until just incorporated. (For best results, add the flour mixture in 3 equal parts.)
4. Spread the batter into the prepared pan. Bake at 350°F for 40-45 minutes or until a toothpick inserted into the center comes out clean. Cool the cake in the pan for 10 minutes before inverting onto a wire rack to cool completely.
5. To prepare the drizzle, stir together the cocoa powder, agave, and milk. Drizzle on top of the cooled cake.

Nutrition Information: 173 calories | 2.6g fat (1.2g saturated fat, 0.8g unsaturated fat) | 18.0mg cholesterol
239.6mg sodium | 33.1g carbohydrates (3.6g fiber, 12.2g sugar) | 6.1g protein

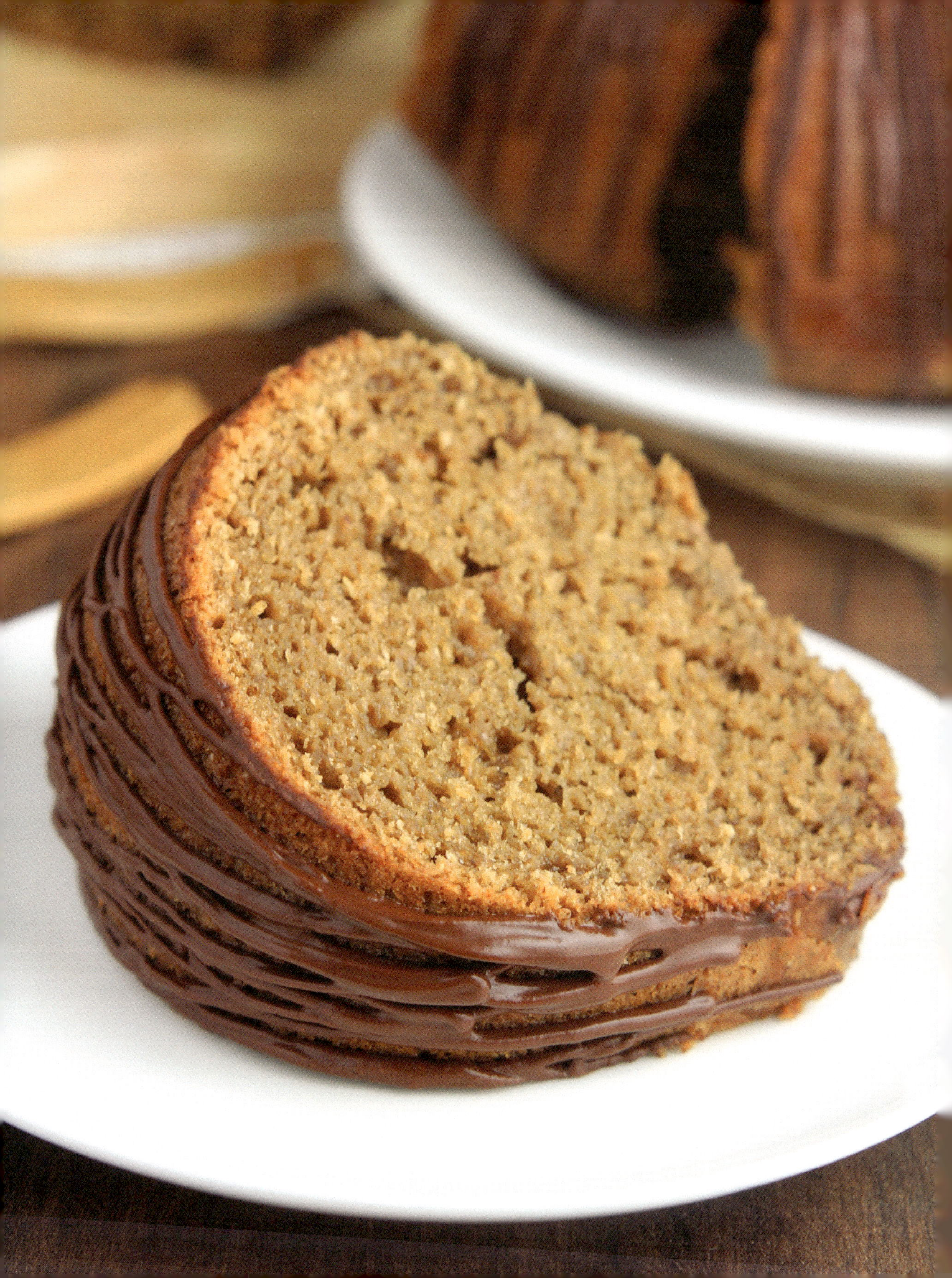

PEANUT BUTTER CUP CHEESECAKE

prep time: 25 minutes ♥ baking time: 43-48 minutes
inactive time: 8 hours ♥ yields: 12 slices

To celebrate special occasions, we sometimes dine at a fancy restaurant chain famous for their cheesecakes. Although the establishment never offers reservations, I rarely mind waiting in the lobby because I love staring at the jam-packed dessert display case. It's full of inspiration for a baking-obsessed blogger! After spotting the peanut butter cup flavor one year, I quickly decided to recreate this lighter version at home.

- 7 full sheets (109g) chocolate graham crackers
- 1 tbsp (14g) unsalted butter, melted and cooled slightly
- 3 large egg whites, room temperature and divided
- 3 (8oz) blocks fat-free cream cheese, room temperature
- ½ cup (96g) granulated sugar
- ½ tbsp (4g) cornstarch
- 1 tbsp (15mL) vanilla extract
- 16 miniature peanut butter cups, diced and frozen

AMY'S ADVICE

I highly recommend dark chocolate peanut butter cups, if you can find them! Freezing the diced peanut butter cups while preparing the rest of the cheesecake helps the pieces stick together when folding them into the filling.

1. Preheat the oven to 300°F, and lightly coat a 9"-round springform pan with nonstick cooking spray.
2. To prepare the crust, add the graham crackers to a food processor, and pulse until they're fine crumbs. Add the crumbs to a small bowl, and mix in the butter and 1 egg white. Press the mixture into the bottom and slightly up the sides of the prepared pan. Bake at 300°F for 8 minutes. Cool completely.
3. To prepare the filling, beat the cream cheese and sugar in a medium bowl until creamy. Mix in the remaining egg whites one at a time. Mix in the cornstarch and vanilla. Fold in the diced peanut butter cups.
4. Spread the filling on top of the cooled crust, and bake at 300°F for 35-40 minutes or until the center barely jiggles when shaken. Cool the cheesecake to room temperature before covering with plastic wrap, ensuring that the plastic completely touches the top of the cheesecake, and chill for at least 8 hours before serving.

HP

Nutrition Information: 195 calories | 4.7g fat (2.0g saturated fat, 2.5g unsaturated fat) | 12.6mg cholesterol
478.7mg sodium | 25.0g carbohydrates (2.0g fiber, 17.6g sugar) | 10.4g protein

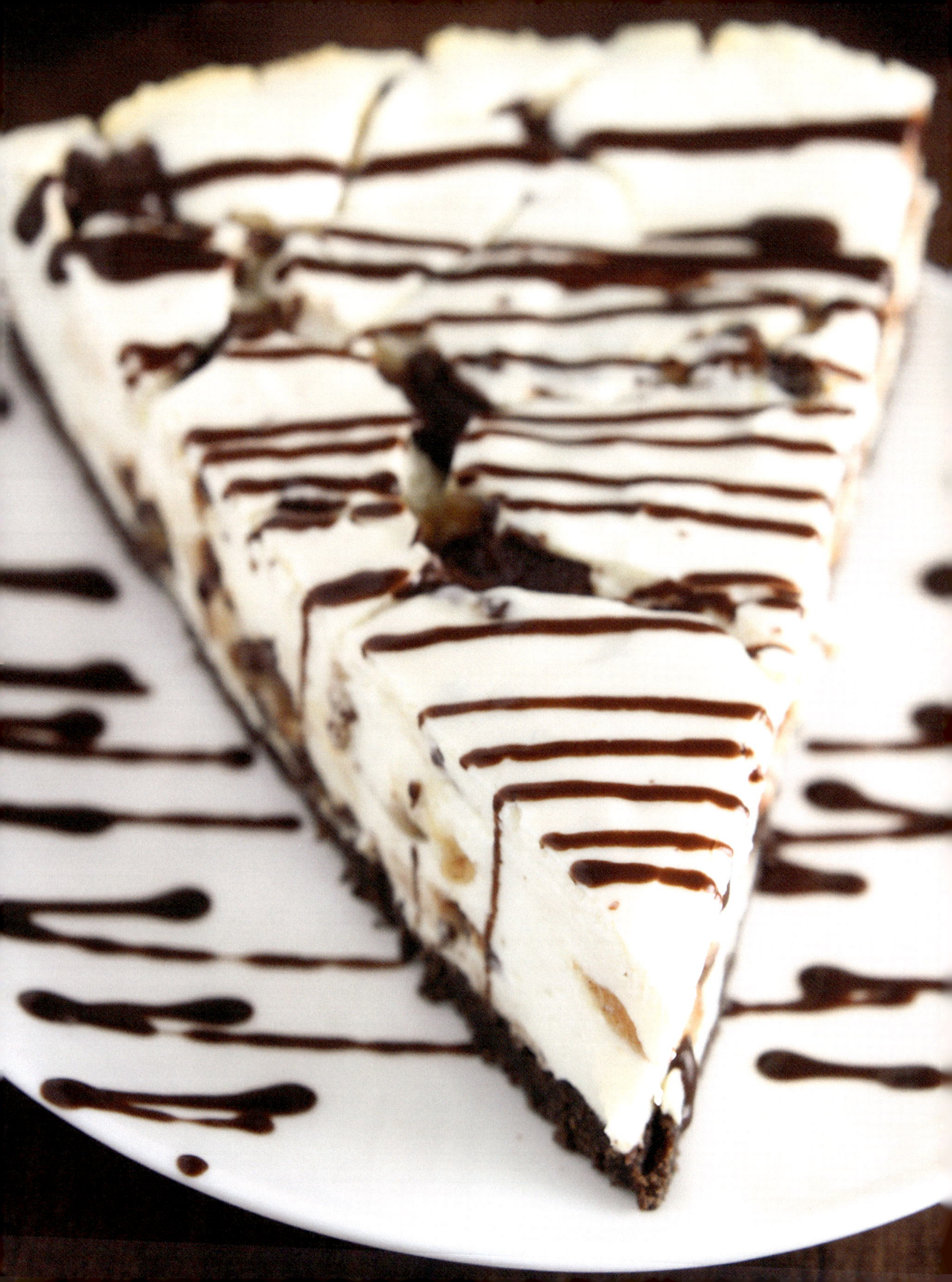

SUBSTITUTIONS AND NUTRITION CLARIFICATIONS

Not everyone can eat all of the ingredients in these recipes! Here is a list of all of the tried-and-true substitutions for many of the treats included in this cookbook. I can only guarantee that these substitutions will work, but if you'd like to try a different substitution that isn't listed here, you're more than welcome to do so. This list also includes clarifications on the Nutrition Information for any recipes with slightly ambiguous ingredients.

BREAKFASTS

Strawberry Banana Chocolate Chip Muffins (P.16)

GF Use the following gluten-free flour blend: 1 cup (120g) millet flour, ½ cup (60g) tapioca flour, ¼ cup (30g) brown rice flour, and 1 ½ teaspoons xanthan gum.

♥ Regular whole wheat, whole wheat pastry, or even all-purpose flour may be substituted in place of the white whole wheat flour. All of the flours except regular whole wheat will produce the same tender texture. Regular whole wheat will be slightly denser.

Double Chocolate Zucchini Muffins (P.18)

GF Use the following gluten-free flour blend: ½ cup (60g) millet flour, ¼ cup (30g) tapioca flour, ¼ cup (30g) brown rice flour, and ¾ teaspoon xanthan gum.

Dark Chocolate Drizzled Blueberry Scones (P.20)

GF Use the following gluten-free flour blend: 1 cup (120g) millet flour, ¼ cup (30g) brown rice flour, ¼ cup (30g) tapioca flour, and 1 ½ teaspoons xanthan gum.

V Substitute Earth Balance buttery sticks in place of the butter; non-dairy milk in place of the nonfat milk; and soy, coconut, or almond yogurt in place of the Greek yogurt.

♥ If using regular dried blueberries, dice them before folding into the dough. They should be about the size of miniature chocolate chips.

Pumpkin Chocolate Chip Scones (P.23)

GF Use the following gluten-free flour blend: 1 cup (120g) millet flour, ¼ cup (30g) brown rice flour, ¼ cup (30g) tapioca flour, and 1 ½ teaspoons xanthan gum.

V Substitute Earth Balance buttery sticks in place of the butter and non-dairy milk in place of the nonfat milk.

Chocolate Chip Buttermilk Pancakes (P.24)

♥ You must use buttermilk in this recipe. It's more acidic than regular milk, which is required to react with the baking soda and baking powder.

♥ As a buttermilk substitute, I highly recommend powdered buttermilk. It's shelf-stable and keeps for ages. Simply mix 2 tablespoons with ½ cup of water to yield the buttermilk required by this recipe. Alternatively, measure out 1 ½ teaspoons of vinegar into a measuring cup, and pour in regular milk (skim, 1%, or 2%) until you reach the ½-cup mark. However, this second method will not yield the same iconic buttermilk flavor.

GF Use the following gluten-free flour blend: ½ cup + 2 tablespoons (75g) millet flour, ¼ cup (30g) tapioca flour, ¼ cup (30g) brown rice flour, and ¾ teaspoon xanthan gum.

Banana French Toast with Chocolate Syrup (P.27)

- **DF** Substitute non-dairy milk in place of the nonfat milk.
- ♥ The Nutrition Information was calculated with Nature's Own® Double Fiber Wheat Bread.

Strawberry & Dark Chocolate Sweet Rolls (P.28)

- ♥ The type of yeast does not matter (regular vs. rapid-rise).
- ♥ Any milk may be substituted in place of the cashew milk.
- ♥ Melted butter may be substituted in place of the coconut oil.
- ♥ White whole wheat flour, whole wheat pastry flour, or all-purpose flour may be substituted in place of the whole wheat flour.
- ♥ For a sweeter drizzle, increase the agave by 1-2 teaspoons and decrease the cashew milk by the same amount until it reaches your desired taste.
- ♥ The Nutrition Information was calculated with 3 cups of whole wheat flour.

Chocolate Fudge Brownie Oatmeal (P.30)

- **GF** Use gluten-free oats.
- **V** Substitute non-dairy milk in place of the nonfat milk.

White Chocolate Berry Cheesecake Oatmeal (P.32)

- **GF** Use gluten-free oats.

Dark Chocolate Cherry Granola (P.34)

- **GF** Use gluten-free oats.
- **V** Substitute 2 tablespoons of non-dairy milk for the egg white.

Dark Chocolate Cherry Yogurt Parfaits (P.37)

- **GF** Use gluten-free oats in the Dark Chocolate Cherry Granola.

- ♥ Any sweetener may be substituted in place of the Truvia®.

White Chocolate Cinnamon Apple Coffee Cake (P.38)

- **C** Substitute chopped dark chocolate or miniature chocolate chips instead.
- **GF** Use millet flour in place of the whole wheat flour in the topping. Use the following gluten-free flour blend for the cake: 1 cup (120g) millet flour, ½ cup (60g) tapioca flour, ¼ cup (30g) brown rice flour, and 1 ½ teaspoons xanthan gum.
- ♥ Whole wheat pastry flour or white whole wheat flour may be substituted in place of the regular whole wheat flour.

Chocolate Covered Strawberry Green Smoothie (P.40)

- **V** Substitute non-dairy milk in place of the nonfat milk.
- ♥ Any sweetener may be substituted in place of the Truvia®.

Skinny Double Chocolate Frappuccino (P.42)

- **V** Substitute non-dairy milk in place of the nonfat milk.
- ♥ Any sweetener may be substituted in place of the Truvia®.

Skinny Cookies 'n Cream Frappuccino (P.45)

- **GF** Use gluten-free chocolate sandwich cookies.
- **V** Substitute non-dairy milk in place of the nonfat milk.

SNACKS

Pumpkin Chocolate Chip Granola Bars (P.50)

- **GF** Use gluten-free oats.
- **V** Substitute non-dairy milk in place of the nonfat milk.

Dark Chocolate Blueberry Granola Bars (P.52)
- **GF** Use gluten-free oats.
- **V** Substitute non-dairy milk in place of the nonfat milk.

Chocolate Date Energy Bites (P.55)
- **GF** Use gluten-free oats.

Chocolate Chip Soft Pretzel Bites (P.56)
- ♥ The Nutrition Information was calculated with 3 ¾ cups of whole wheat flour and without the wash or sea salt.

Chocolate Kettle Corn (P.58)
- ♥ Any butter or oil may be substituted for the coconut oil.

Dark Chocolate Cinnamon Muddy Buddies (P.60)
- **V** Substitute non-dairy milk in place of the nonfat milk.
- ♥ The Nutrition Information was calculated with 6 tablespoons of powdered sugar.

Circus Animal Snack Mix (P.62)
- ♥ The Nutrition Information was calculated with Danielle Honey Banana Chips.

Chocolate Pretzel GORP (P.63)
- **GF** Use gluten-free miniature pretzel twists.

Strawberry Dip with Chocolate Bear Dunkers (P.64)
- ♥ Frozen unsweetened strawberries that have been thawed and drained may be substituted for the fresh strawberries.

Strawberry Hazelnut Quesadillas (P.65)
- ♥ The Nutrition Information was calculated with Mission® Whole Wheat Tortillas.

Chocolate Elvis Sandwiches (P.67)
- **V** Substitute agave or maple syrup in place of the honey and non-dairy milk in place of the nonfat milk.
- ♥ The Nutrition Information was calculated with Nature's Own® Double Fiber Wheat Bread.

Cocoa Sugar Tortilla Chips (P.68)
- ♥ The Nutrition Information was calculated with Mission® Whole Wheat Tortillas.

Mini Strawberry "Pizza" Bagels (P.71)
- ♥ The Nutrition Information was calculated with Thomas'® 100% Whole Wheat Mini Bagels.

Chocolate & Granola Apple Nachos (P.72)
- **GF** Use gluten-free oats.
- **V** Substitute non-dairy milk for the nonfat milk.

DESSERTS
Chocolate Chip Cookies (P.76)
- **GF** Use the following gluten-free flour blend: ½ cup (60g) millet flour, ½ cup (60g) tapioca flour, 6 tablespoons (42g) coconut flour, and 1 ½ teaspoons xanthan gum.

Oatmeal Chocolate Chip Cookies (P.81)
- **GF** Use gluten-free oats and the following gluten-free flour blend: ½ cup (60g) millet flour, 2 tablespoons (15g) tapioca flour, 2 tablespoons (15g) brown rice flour, and ½ teaspoon xanthan gum.
- ♥ Honey or maple syrup may be substituted in place of the agave. The same amount of brown sugar plus an additional ¼ cup of milk may also be substituted.
- ♥ Chopped dark chocolate may be substituted in place of the chocolate chips.

Fudgy Dark Chocolate Brownies (P.84)
- **GF** Use the following gluten-free flour blend: ½ cup (60g) millet flour, 2 tablespoons (15g) tapioca flour, 2 tablespoons (15g) brown rice flour, and ½ teaspoon xanthan gum.

Fudgy Caramel Brownies (P.87)
- **GF** Use the following gluten-free flour blend: ½ cup (60g) millet flour, 2 tablespoons (15g) tapioca flour, 2 tablespoons (15g) brown rice flour, and ½ teaspoon xanthan gum.
- ♥ The Nutrition Information was calculated with Smucker's® Sundae Syrup™ Caramel Flavored Syrup.

Caramel Seven Layer Bars (P.88)
- ♥ If you do not have Truvia®, substitute 1 tablespoon of sugar or the equivalent of your favorite no-calorie sweetener.
- ♥ Digestive biscuits may be substituted for the graham crackers.
- ♥ The Nutrition Information was calculated with Let's Do … Organic® Reduced Fat Shredded Coconut.

Strawberry Frosted Chocolate Cereal Treats (P.90)
- ♥ Any granulated sweetener, including regular sugar, may be substituted for the granulated sucralose.

S'mores Cheesecake Bars (P.93)
- ♥ The Nutrition Information was calculated with HERSHEY'S® Chocolate Syrup.

Dark Chocolate Raspberry Truffles (P.94)
- **V** Substitute agave in place of the honey.

Mini White Chocolate Berry Lemon Parfaits (P.98)
- ♥ Any granulated sweetener, including regular sugar, may be substituted for the granulated sucralose.

Strawberry & Chocolate Whipped Cream Crêpes (P.101)
- **GF** Use the following gluten-free flour blend: ½ cup (60g) millet flour, ¼ cup (30g) tapioca flour, 2 tablespoons (15g) brown rice flour, and ¾ teaspoon xanthan gum.
- ♥ Regular powdered sugar may be substituted for the Confectioners Style Swerve®.

Chocolate Pudding Pie (P.102)
- ♥ Cow's milk generally performs the best and allows the pudding to thicken the best. Do
- **GF** not substitute soy milk. Follow the directions on the package for any other milk substitutions.

Dark Chocolate Strawberry Crumble (P.105)
- **GF** Use certified gluten-free old-fashioned oats.
- **V** Substitute coconut oil or Earth Balance buttery spread.
- ♥ Honey or maple syrup may be substituted in place of the agave.
- ♥ The Nutrition Information was calculated without the ice cream for serving.
- ♥ The crumb topping is incredibly dark, similar to the taste of 75%+ dark chocolate. For a lighter taste, substitute 1-2 tablespoons of whole wheat flour or millet flour for the equivalent amount of cocoa powder.

Mocha Ice Cream Float (P.107)
- **V** Substitute non-dairy chocolate ice cream.
- ♥ The Nutrition Information was calculated with DREYER'S Slow Churned® No Sugar Added Triple Chocolate Ice Cream.

Sugar Cookie Chocolate Ice Cream Sandwiches (P.108)
- ♥ The Nutrition Information was calculated with DREYER'S Slow Churned® No Sugar Added Triple Chocolate Ice Cream.

Mini Dark Chocolate Lava Cakes (P.111)
- **GF** Use the following gluten-free flour blend: 2 tablespoons (15g) millet flour, 1 tablespoon (7g) tapioca flour, 1 tablespoon (7g) brown rice flour, and ⅛ teaspoon xanthan gum.
- ♥ The Nutrition Information was calculated

with 4 small squares of Trader Joe's® 72% Dark Chocolate.

Chocolate Strawberry Shortcakes (P.112)
GF Use the following gluten-free flour blend: 1 cup (120g) millet flour, ½ cup (60g) tapioca flour, ¼ cup (30g) brown rice flour, and 1 ½ teaspoons xanthan gum.

Coconut Cake with Dark Chocolate Frosting (P.118)
GF Use the following gluten-free flour blend: 1 cup (120g) millet flour, ½ cup (60g) tapioca flour, ¼ cup (30g) brown rice flour, and 1 ¼ teaspoons xanthan gum.

♥ Dark chocolate chips may be substituted for the chopped dark chocolate.

Dark Chocolate Drizzled Coffee Bundt Cake (P.120)
GF Use the following gluten-free flour blend: 1 ½ cups (180g) millet flour, ¾ cup (90g) tapioca flour, ¾ cup (90g) brown rice flour, and 2 ¼ teaspoons xanthan gum.

Peanut Butter Cup Cheesecake (P.122)
GF Substitute gluten-free chocolate cookies.

ACKNOWLEDGEMENTS

Although chocolate appears to be the most important ingredient in these recipes, that award actually belongs to a group of very loving and supportive people who made this cookbook possible.

Firstly, to a pair of warm and welcoming local television news anchors who helped plant the idea of publishing a cookbook. Although I had considered writing one in the past, it was the encouragement from Cody and Melissa that propelled me forward to put the idea into motion.

Secondly, to my blogging friends, many of whom have already written their own cookbooks. They took an interest in my journey, provided valuable advice, and cheered me on. Jessica, Dorothy, Trish, Karen, Ashley, and the other Sac ladies and Bay Area bloggers—thank you so much.

Thirdly, to my taste tester friends who always provided honest and helpful feedback. It takes a special type of person to sample four batches of chocolate chip cookies in the same day and still save room for brownies and cheesecake, too. Andrea, Rachel and family, Camellia, and the Caltech crew—I couldn't have done this without you.

Fourthly, to the talented lady who designed this cookbook's layout and patiently answered my emails at all hours of the day and night. Sarah, you have a wonderful gift, and I am so grateful for your valuable help and advice.

Finally, to my family and my guy who have always loved me, encouraged me, and believed in me. With the countless early mornings, late nights, and long baking-filled days in between, your encouragement kept me going through the entire process of recipe testing, photography, and writing. I wouldn't be the woman I am today without any of you, so from the very bottom of my heart, thank you.

ABOUT THE AUTHOR

Amy is the author of the popular blog *Amy's Healthy Baking*, where she publishes plenty of sweet breakfast, snack, and dessert recipes like the ones included in this cookbook. When she isn't baking, photographing, or washing the ensuing mountain of dirty dishes, Amy loves to exercise (to balance out all of those treats!), spend time with her family, and travel around the country to watch Major League Baseball games. She and her dad have visited twenty-two stadiums so far!

Follow Amy and her healthier baking adventures for all of her delicious recipes and exclusive behind-the-scenes sneak peeks.

BLOG: amyshealthybaking.com
INSTAGRAM: @AmysHealthyBaking and @AmyBakesHealthy
FACEBOOK: facebook.com/AmysHealthyBaking
PINTEREST: pinterest.com/AmyBakesHealthy
TWITTER: @AmyBakesHealthy

Remember to tag your cookbook recipe pictures with #healthierchocolatetreats!

Happy baking!

CPSIA information can be obtained
at www.ICGtesting.com
Printed in the USA
LVIC04n0003071115
461314LV00003B/3